Occasional Papers Number 2

CONFLICT AT MONMOUTH COURT HOUSE

Edited by Mary R. Murrin and Richard Waldron

Proceedings of a Symposium
Commemorating the Two-Hundredth
Anniversary of the Battle of Monmouth

April 8, 1978

Trenton
New Jersey Historical Commission
              Department of State
Monmouth County Historical Association
1983

New Jersey Historical Commission
113 West State Street, CN 305
Trenton, NJ 08625

Department of State
Thomas H. Kean, Governor
Jane Burgio, Secretary of State

Library of Congress Cataloging in Publication Data

Main entry under title:

Conflict at Monmouth Court House.

    (Occasional Papers / New Jersey Historical Commission; no. 2)
    Papers presented at a symposium sponsored by the Monmouth County Historical Association, the Monmouth County Heritage Committee, and the New Jersey Historical Commission.
    Bibliography: p.
    1. Monmouth, Battle of, 1778—Congresses. 2. Lee, Charles, 1731-1782—Congresses. I. Murrin, Mary R. II. Waldron, Richard, 1945-   . III. Monmouth County Historical Association. IV. Monmouth County Heritage Committee. V. New Jersey Historical Commission. VI. Series: Occasional papers (New Jersey Historical Commission); no. 2.
E241.M7C73   973.3'34   81-18700
ISBN 0-89743-054-9

CONTENTS

INTRODUCTION

Of all the battles of the Revolutionary War none is more ambiguous than the battle of Monmouth. It is often cited as a major turning point in the fortunes of the United States and the Continental army. Because the Continental Line fought British regulars on an equal footing for the first time, historians see Monmouth as the battle which marked the coming of age of Washington's army and—somehow—a mature commitment of the people of the United States to the revolutionary cause. Yet it is not clear which side, if either, won the battle, and there is scant evidence that Monmouth had any salutary effect on rebel morale. Even George Washington admitted that the "glorious and happy day" had evolved from an "unfortunate, and bad beginning." The British commander in the field that day, Sir Henry Clinton, scoffed at the notion of a rebel victory. His memoirs dismissed Monmouth in a terse description of a minor skirmish that caused the king's army little discomfort. Since neither Washington nor Clinton was an impartial observer, they are entitled to hold conflicting views. But the fact remains that Monmouth has caused historians at least as much interpretive and factual difficulty as any other battle of the American Revolution.

Added to the genteel discussion of the battle's place in the context of the Revolutionary War is a more passionate debate about the conduct of Charles Lee, commander of the American advance guard at Monmouth. Did Lee disobey orders and nearly cost the Continentals a victory—a victory achieved at the last moment by Washington's timely intervention? Or did Lee follow his orders in both letter and spirit only to be betrayed by the inactivity of his subordinates and Washington's lack of speed in moving to his support? Was Charles Lee a traitor, a scapegoat or merely an incompetent?

This volume assesses all these questions. The papers were originally presented at "The Battle of Monmouth: A Commemorative Symposium," on April 8, 1978. The symposium was sponsored by the Monmouth County Historical Association, the Monmouth County Heritage Committee, and the New Jersey Historical Commission.

Mark E. Lender's "The Battle of Monmouth in the Military Context of the American Revolution" describes the entire Monmouth campaign: the British evacuation of Philadelphia in mid-June 1778, the convergent marches of the enemy armies across New Jersey, the battle, and the successful British escape to Sandy Hook and thence to New York City. Lender concludes that the battle did mark a sort of maturity for both the Continental army and the New Jersey militia, and that its dramatic aftermath, the court-martial of Charles Lee, made future public criticism of Washington, as commander in chief, virtually impossible.

In "Heroines All: The Plight of Women at War in America, 1776-1778," Elizabeth

Evans depicts the rigors endured by the women who accompanied both armies from the beginning of the war to the battle of Monmouth. These women performed duties both military—witness any number of Molly Pitchers—and nonmilitary. They included representatives of every social stratum, from titled wives of Hessian generals to laundresses who starved and froze with the Continentals at Valley Forge.

In his comments on these papers James Kirby Martin finds Lender's presentation to be an excellent overview of the battle organized along the lines of Washington or Lee, good or bad. Suggesting the need for a fresh perspective—the conflict from the British side—he briefly analyses why the war was virtually unwinnable for the British. In contrast, he chides Evans for an anecdotal presentation rather than a meaningful examination of the position of an important group. Offering his own brief analysis of the position of women in the army, Martin concludes with a call for additional work on the subject.

The symposium's afternoon session was devoted to Charles Lee and his actions at Monmouth. Dennis P. Ryan set the stage with "Lee Before Monmouth: A Reappraisal of His Military Career," a portrait, often in Lee's own words, of a vain, ambitious and able man whose acid tongue and ill-temper made him his own worst enemy. Ryan concludes that Lee's behavior at Monmouth "conformed to the pattern of his long career as British officer, Whig politician and American general."

"Charles Lee's Actions at the Battle of Monmouth" is a set of related papers presented by a panel of distinguished military historians, chaired by Samuel S. Smith. Smith introduces the topic with a succinct account of the events of the Monmouth campaign and the charges against Lee at his court-martial.

Russell F. Weigley, in "Washington's Strategic Intentions for the Battle of Monmouth," describes the Continental army as the last viable entity of a revolution that was slowly expiring as a political and spiritual movement. Washington, aware of the symbolic importance of his army, had preserved it throughout the war by avoiding a general engagement with the British. At Monmouth he seems to have abandoned this prudent course, and Weigley argues that Lee's caution saved Washington from himself by averting a potentially disastrous confrontation with the enemy. The Continental army thus remained intact and the Revolution could struggle on for another three years until it was salvaged by the historical accident of Yorktown.

Roy K. Flint, in "Lifting the Fog of Battle: Charles Lee at the Battle of Monmouth," assesses Lee's activities in light of the modern military theory of an army's movement to contact its enemy. Flint concludes that Lee, given the time and information he had available, did all that one could expect of an advance guard commander.

In "The Traitorous Charles Lee," Kemble Widmer describes Lee's career in the Continental army as marked by perfidy. Widmer states flatly that Lee was a traitor, from his capture by the British in 1776 through his part in the battle of Monmouth.

The proceedings conclude with Robert F. Benthuysen's essay "They Were There: The Battle of Monmouth Through Participants' Eyes. A Selected Bibliography of Printed Sources." Van Benthuysen describes eyewitness accounts by Americans, British and Hessians, and enlivens his discussion with well-chosen quotations from the participants in the battle.

The editors are grateful to a number of people who worked to make the symposium a success and to ready this volume for publication. Charles T. Lyle, former director of the Monmouth County Historical Association, who conceived the idea for the program, was helpful at every stage of its planning. Elsalyn P. Drucker, formerly the Association's librarian, handled the symposium's logistics with skill and aplomb. The late George Goodfellow, then chairman of the Monmouth County Heritage Committee, was a constant source of support and encouragement. The editors also wish to thank Diane E. Kauffman, Judith A. Fullerton, Adele M. Presha and the personnel of the New Jersey Department of Education's Word Processing Center for typing the manuscript, as well as Peggy K. Lewis for thoughtful editorial work at all stages of publication, and Nancy H. Dallaire for meticulous and considered design of the text and cover.

THE BATTLE OF MONMOUTH
IN THE MILITARY CONTEXT
OF THE AMERICAN REVOLUTION

Mark Edward Lender

Early on the morning of May 24, 1778, General Sir William Howe formally relinquished his post as commander of the British army in America to his successor, Lieutenant General Sir Henry Clinton. There were no elaborate change-of-command ceremonies, just some emotional good-byes from brother officers before taking ship for home. Howe himself was subdued: unhappy for some time in his office, he had longed to give it up, and he was visibly relieved when orders arrived directing his return to England. But he was returning under a cloud—his reputation, built on victories around New York in 1776, now lay tarnished by the affairs at Trenton and Princeton and by the disastrous results of the campaigns of 1777. The disappointments of that year, which saw the loss of General John Burgoyne's entire army at Saratoga, were not all his fault. By eighteenth-century standards Howe was certainly competent enough, and after heavy fighting he had managed to take the rebel capital of Philadelphia.[1] Nevertheless, Howe had neither crushed the Revolution nor finished off the battered Continental army, and critics at home were asking why. It was thus not a joyous homecoming that

The author gratefully acknowledges the assistance of Lyn Michalski in preparing this essay.

awaited him, and Horace Walpole's observation that the general had come back "much richer in money than in laurels" was on the mark.[2]

Walpole's quip, however, applied equally to the general British war effort, for so far it too had produced few laurels. In fact, 1777 had been one of the most catastrophic years in the annals of British arms. Not only had Burgoyne been lost, but from the vantage of early 1778 even Howe's capture of Philadelphia appeared to have been a Pyrrhic victory. Soon after the fall of the rebel capital, France had entered the war—a result in part of the debacle at Saratoga and of Washington's stiff resistance in Pennsylvania—and forced London to reassess its strategic prospects. The ministry soberly concluded that England could not fight everywhere at once and so ordered a redeployment of some of the troops in the Middle Colonies to meet commitments in other, more vital sectors of the empire. Given the reduced number of troops available for duty in the region, London also concluded that Philadelphia, won at the cost of considerable bloodshed and valor the year before, was no longer tenable; and on March 21 orders went out (they reached the city on May 23) directing the new British commander to take the army back to New York. The plan made sense given the altered military context of 1778; but to the army the thought of surrendering the town without firing a shot was a final humiliation.[3] The only real victory of 1777 had turned to ashes.

This British strategic readjustment, of which the evacuation of Philadelphia was only a part, marked the end of a distinct phase of the war. Further plans to seek a decision in the Middle Colonies were dropped in favor of a thrust into the American South, where local sentiment and strategic considerations seemingly promised better results than a continued struggle in the North. Moreover, there was some hope that a new peace initiative announced by the ministry in March would make further combat unnecessary. Alarmed over the losses of 1777 and by the new war with France, Britain was ready to grant the rebels virtual self-rule provided they retained their allegiance to the crown. But even if the peace overture failed (as it quickly did), there was to be no more futile chasing of Washington's elusive Continentals. Once Philadelphia and the fields of 1777 were behind them—or so the new British view held—the redcoats could be employed elsewhere to considerably more profit.[4]

Before the king's generals could bring their frustrating northern war to a finish, though, the Americans were to give it an unplanned final episode. Rather than allow the Royal Army to abandon Philadelphia and return to New York unmolested, the patriots struck the retreating redcoats in late June near the village of Freehold in central New Jersey. In an act of supreme irony, this fiercely contested action—the battle of Monmouth—saw Washington nearly give the British at the last minute something they had vainly sought for the past two years, a showdown general engagement. One of the most dramatic battles of the war, the fight set something of a record for sustained combat on a single day. And when the clash had ended, it was clear that more than British strategy had changed since 1777: the Americans too had formed some notions of their own on the conduct of the war, and aspects of what they had learned were boldly in evidence during the Monmouth affair. For those who looked deeply enough at the results of the battle, the clear signs that the soldier and civilian rebels had matured con-

siderably in their mastery and understanding of warfare boded ill for the crown no matter how it chose to press its side of the war in the future. This essay will reexamine this already much-studied and well-known battle and suggest how some of its more important aspects, and their implications, can deepen our understanding of the broader military context of the Revolution.

The Armies of 1778

Henry Clinton took no particular pleasure in assuming his new command. Forty years old and generally known as a tough leader, he had previously done fairly well in the field against the patriots and had even distinguished himself at Bunker Hill. Now he wanted nothing more than to face Washington in a head-to-head confrontation, one in which he was sure he would smash the American. His command held some of the best regiments of British and Hessian regulars in the army, most of them solid veterans, plus a number of Loyalist battalions; altogether he had some seventeen thousand men. Splendidly trained, they were also in excellent physical condition after spending the winter on the lines outside Philadelphia. Under these circumstances Clinton, like the rest of the army, considered a withdrawal without at least an effort against the Continentals ridiculous and shameful—and hardly the way to begin a new assignment.[5] "No officer," he wrote in disgust, "who had the least anxious regard for his professional fame would court a change so hopeless as this now appeared likely to be."[6] Had he been free to pursue his own designs, there is little doubt that the spring of 1778 would have found him moving toward the rebels, not away from them.

The general, though, was anything but free. His orders, already waiting for him when he took over Howe's job, specifically directed him to quit the city and get his command to New York, where he would then join forces with the Royal Navy in harassing patriot coastal towns. He was, as well, to dispatch a sizeable contingent of his troops to reinforce British positions in the West Indies and Florida. The government also noted the importance of Philadelphia and added that Clinton might try holding it if he was strong enough after executing the rest of his orders. But everyone knew this was impossible. Besides, Clinton had no time to do more than get out of town quickly. In early June he learned that a French fleet was heading for Delaware Bay, and if his soldiers were to use the Delaware as an escape route, they had no time to waste.[7]

Clinton had indeed intended to leave via the Delaware; but the navy, he found, had too few transports to carry both his troops and a sizeable number of Tories who preferred flight to staying behind in Philadelphia. Under the circumstances, he assigned his sick and wounded, military dependents, the Tories, and some Hessian units he felt were on the verge of deserting to the available ships, and prepared to march the bulk of the soldiery (about thirteen thousand men) across New Jersey.[8] The prospect of the adventure, which he guessed could take as much as three weeks, actually had some bright spots in the general's view. First, the overland route would take less time than the trip by sea, and it would forestall the possibility of a surprise Continental attack on New York, then defended by only a small garrison. Second, and best of all, there was always the possibility that Washington could be drawn into a fight.[9] Thus, throughout late May and early June, the British loaded ships and ferried baggage and advance units to a New Jersey bridgehead at Cooper's Creek; and finally, without any patriot interference, the remaining troops crossed the river early on June 18. The transports dropped down river several hours later. The British were gone, and the prize of 1777 had become, quite peacefully, an American city once more.

On the east bank of the Delaware, Clinton divided his command into two columns. Major General Charles, Lord Cornwallis led the main body, including a heavily escorted baggage train, which struck out on the main road toward Allentown, some forty miles northeast. General Alexander Leslie headed the other column, which kept to roads within supporting distance of the main group. And on all sides of Clinton's men rode a screening force of some seven hundred dragoons, excellent troops who served as the army's eyes, as well as providing it with security against surprise. Moving ever deeper into hostile territory, these British units were a force to be reckoned with.

The patriots, in the meantime, had been anticipating Clinton's movement. Still in his winter encampment at Valley Forge, Washington initially had no idea of what the British planned for the spring, but he did what he could to guard against all contingencies.[10] In early May, the commander in chief sent Brigadier General William Maxwell into New Jersey with his New Jersey Continentals. Maxwell was to gather intelligence and harass the flanks of any enemy incursion (and since the British capture of Philadelphia, they had raided across the Delaware several times).[11] As the tempo of Clinton's evacuation preparations increased, Maxwell quickly got word back to Washington; and by late May the commanding general, though not fully convinced, believed increasingly that the British were going to move across the Delaware. As a precaution, he ordered some of his subordinates to get ready to cross the river themselves and urged the Jersey Continentals to extra vigilance.[12] This was advice that Maxwell really did not need: if the British came into New Jersey, no one had to tell him that their probable path would lead right through his present position. In fact, by June 6 the Jersey Brigade commander was already edgy: convinced that trouble was imminent, he reported that he was preparing his men to meet it. He also warned local civilians to get their livestock and furniture out of harm's way.[13] The Americans therefore knew approximately what was coming—the only questions remaining were exactly where and when the enemy would move.

In the event of an invasion, Washington hoped that Maxwell and state militia forces would be able to slow Clinton enough for the rest of the rebel army to catch him. With this in view, the commander in chief asked Major General Philemon Dickinson, commander of the New Jersey militia, to rally his men and join forces with Maxwell to harass and impede any British march. Dickinson, who was probably one of the best militia officers of the war, already had some men in the field, and he quickly went to work raising more and organizing them to work with the Continentals.[14] To assist in the mobilization, the New-Jersey Gazette notified all militiamen "to be particularly attentive to signals, as a movement of the enemy is soon expected"; and following this alert, Dickinson asked Governor William Livingston to order out all of the state's citizen-soldiers. Livingston declined this extreme step, which would have left the rest of the state defenseless (and many of the militia from the far northern and southern counties were too far away to respond effectively anyway); but on June 16 he called up half of the local forces, who were to join those already in the field.[15]

Sensing the urgency of the situation, the militia troops began turning out. In fact, they moved into action faster and in greater numbers than at any other time since New Jersey's first flush of enthusiasm for the war in early 1776. By the time Clinton had started his march, Dickinson commanded about a thousand men and his strength was growing.[16] New Jersey, which in past crises had not mobilized its military resources effectively, had this time reacted quickly and with relative efficiency.

Above Philadelphia, word that Clinton had finally begun his awaited march electrified the men at Valley Forge. Washington, however, while anxious to respond effectively to developments with his Continental regulars, was not sure what to do. The Continentals were a force substantially improved in almost every respect over their status the previous year. Many of the men were now tried veterans, part of the long term standing army the commander in chief had wanted since the beginning of the war. The spring of 1778 found them better equipped than ever before (the fruit of the French alliance), and General Friedrich von Steuben had spent the Valley Forge winter drilling the regiments in the linear tactics he had practiced in the Prussian army of Frederick the Great. Little by little, Washington was molding into a reality his personal dream of an army capable of facing the redcoats on their own terms. But although even Clinton admitted that the rebels looked stronger than ever, no one—British or American—was ready to suggest that the Continentals could at this point hold their own in an open battle against the cream of the British army (which was exactly what Clinton had with him).[17] Conse-

quently, before Clinton's intention to leave Philadelphia became known, in early May a council of war had recommended, with the endorsement of Washington and most of the senior officer corps, that the Continental Line adopt a defensive posture in the coming campaign and react to enemy initiatives rather than immediately go over to the attack.[18]

This caution was evident among many of the officers at last faced with the prospect of chasing a withdrawing Clinton. At a council of war on June 17, Washington learned how divided his officers were on the subject. Some of them, including Steuben and Major General Charles Lee, remained convinced that their regiments were still no match for Clinton's, and that bringing on a general engagement would be "almost criminal." Other generals, notably Anthony Wayne, Nathanael Greene, John Cadwalader, and the young Marquis de Lafayette, were all for attacking in strength. Greene was even willing to risk a major showdown; if it came, he said, then shoot it out.[19] It was thus a divided council that heard of the British march later in the morning; and Washington found himself forced to act without his generals in concert and without formulating a specific plan of operation.

There is little doubt that the rebel commander wanted to be in a position to hit the British, or at least part of them, if the opportunity arose. Hoping that Maxwell and Dickinson would slow Clinton's columns enough for his Continentals to catch them, he got his army on the move. Placing Benedict Arnold in charge of a reoccupied Philadelphia, he then saw General Lee out of camp with the American advance units on the morning of the 19th. Lee crossed the Delaware into New Jersey at Coryell's Ferry (Lambertville) above Trenton on the 20th, and Washington followed him over with the rest of the army on the 21st and 22nd.[20] The chase was on.

The Road to Monmouth

As the majority of the Continentals were moving back into New Jersey for the first time in a year, the detachments of regulars and militia under Maxwell and Dickinson were already seeing action along the British line of march. Together, they hovered on the flanks of the retreating column, picking up deserters, felling trees across the enemy path, destroying bridges and searching for opportunities to ambush detached parties. There was no major fighting, but even before Washington had passed the Delaware the rebels made a brief stand at Mount Holly. At that point the American force put up only token resistence at a narrow gap in the hills before giving way.[21]

The incident at Mount Holly evidently impressed Sir Henry more than it did the Americans. Had the patriot units made a more determined effort to hold the pass, they could have given the British a much tougher time; for the rebel position, as the royal commander noted, was well chosen and easily defended. As it was, Clinton was relieved that a real fight had not developed.[22] Certainly he was anything but afraid of a larger action; his dragoons alone were capable of handling anything the patriots could send against him. But his march was making poor time, and the general was aware that even brief rebel annoyances slowed him even further.

Indeed, the speed of the withdrawal had become a genuine concern. The American harassment was, as Clinton admitted, having its effects. After Mount Holly, he found that the rebels had destroyed "every bridge on our road"; worse, even nature seemed to favor the king's enemies. The roads were often poor, and "as the country is intersected with marshy rivulets," the general noted, "the obstructions we met with were frequent."[23] As the men struggled forward in heavy woolen uniforms and carrying eighty-pound packs, "excessive heat" and torrential rains took turns punishing them. Clouds of mosquitoes added a dimension of discomfort that only those who have endured their peculiar abilities to torture a human being can appreciate. But the impact on the men was only part of the problem. Clinton's baggage train, with tons of vital supplies, also encumbered the army. The hundreds of wagons stretched over twelve miles, and despite a strong guard under Hessian General Wilhelm von Knyphausen, the English commander understood the vulnerability of this critical segment of his column.[24]

The slow pace of the army also made it relatively easy for deserters to slip away. The militia reported picking them up throughout the British passage across the state; in the first week alone Clinton lost several hundred men this way (mostly Hessians, who had formed attachments among Pennsylvania's large German population).[25]

Washington observed the enemy's slow advance with grim satisfaction. Hoping to keep the pressure on Clinton after the initial exchange of shots at Mount Holly, the commander in chief decided to reinforce the troops already clinging to the British flanks. He dispatched a contingent of light horse and Colonel Daniel Morgan's riflemen, whose long-range weapons had done such telling work against Burgoyne at Saratoga.[26] As a consequence, American formations soon operated on virtually every quarter of the British advance. And while there were no large clashes—probably because the hardworking British dragoons discouraged any major Whig efforts to get at Clinton's main body—there was no mistaking the increased American presence: sniping and more ruined bridges and felled trees continued to plague the redcoat columns. On the 23rd a nasty skirmish took place at Crosswicks, when rebel militia and New Jersey Continentals challenged the British at a river crossing. The brief engagement cost Clinton several killed and wounded in a cavalry charge across the river. The Whigs again broke off and withdrew before a larger affair could develop.[27] Beset, then, by the elements and the Americans (probably in that order) Clinton's command arrived at Allentown, thirteen miles southeast of Princeton, on June 24. In almost a week's march the British had covered only some forty miles, a pace of well under ten miles a day. Indeed, after an overland march also seriously impeded by the weather, Washington's main body had been able to close the distance on its slower opponent and on the 24th rested only six miles northwest of Princeton at Hopewell. This left barely twenty miles between the armies, a circumstance demanding some hard decisions from the rival commanders.

With its arrival at Allentown, Sir Henry Clinton's army had reached a literal and figurative crossroads. Until that time, the British general had avoided a decision on which route to take across the rest of New Jersey. Two paths were open to him, and now he had to choose. One road ran northeast from Allentown, through New Brunswick, across the Raritan River and on to Perth Amboy, where his men could cross to safety on Staten Island. The other road took a more southerly course, proceeding through the village of Freehold and on to Sandy Hook, from which the Royal Navy could ferry the army to New York. After considering the situation, Clinton chose the second alternative. To have attempted to cross the Raritan, he noted later in a letter to Lord George Germain, would have invited an attack on his baggage train (which he was convinced Washington was after) when he was in midstream and least able to strike back. Besides, he said, Washington was gathering militia strength to the north, and General Horatio Gates was reportedly also marching to the Raritan from New York State with yet another rebel force.[28] On the other hand, the road to Sandy Hook offered a safer retreat, especially once the column gained the high ground near Middletown. And, as Theodore Thayer has noted, Clinton also reasoned that the more favorable terrain along the southerly route would work to his advantage if, unexpectedly, Washington offered battle.[29] Accordingly, the British commander ordered the movement toward Sandy Hook.

Early on June 25, Clinton's men moved out of Allentown in the direction of Freehold. Knyphausen led the supply train out first (in an effort to get it as far ahead of the Americans as possible) while the rest of the units followed. As usual, the ever-vigilant dragoons ranged protectively on the army's flanks, keeping the lurking rebels at a respectful distance. Unmolested, the king's troops reached Freehold on the afternoon of June 26, when they stopped for a much-needed rest.

While Clinton was deciding to turn toward Sandy Hook, Washington was also pondering his next move. For the American general, however, the options were not as clear. He pressed Maxwell and Dickinson hard for intelligence on Clinton's movements, but he was unable to learn his opponent's destination prior to the British departure from Allentown.[30] Now certain of the enemy path, the commander in chief turned to the question of an assault on at least part of the retreating army. Some of his information indicated that the British might try to bring on a general engagement, but Washington still wanted to avoid this; instead, he sought a plan that would allow him to strike an effective blow at Clinton without risking his own battalions in a major fight. With this end in view, Washington convened a council of war on reaching Hopewell (June 24).[31] Rather than producing any strategic consensus, however, the council served only to air the differences then rending the upper reaches of the Continental army command.

A group of officers around General Nathanael Greene—men like Anthony Wayne and Alexander Hamilton—argued strongly, as they had on June 17, for hitting the enemy as hard as possible, short of bringing on a general engagement (which they would have risked if circumstances looked favorable). Greene later explained that the issue went well beyond purely military considerations. He wrote Washington that the honor of American arms and patriot morale demanded action. "If we suffer the enemy to pass through New Jersey without attacking," he warned, "I think we shall . . . regret it." Remaining passive, the young hawk insisted, would "magnify our deficiencies beyond realities . . . . People expect something from us and our strength demands it. I am by no means for rash measures," he concluded, "but we must preserve our reputation."[32] Lafayette, another fire-eater, agreed. It "would be disgraceful and humiliating," he told the council, "to allow the enemy to cross the Jerseys in tranquility."[33] The argument was compelling; Washington was still smarting from criticisms of his generalship during the campaigns of 1776 and 1777, and now he badly wanted to strike a telling blow. And as this advice was coming from some of his most talented subordinates, the aggressive course sorely tempted the commander in chief.

Equally insistent, however, was a coterie of officers who supported the opposing views of General Lee. Lee was a special case in the army. He was a British veteran with ardent republican beliefs and Congress had appointed him second in command early in the war. Brilliant in the first months of the conflict, he became increasingly critical of Washington's mistakes in the dark days of 1776. His capture in December of that year probably saved the Continental command a serious break between its two senior generals.[34] Held prisoner for fifteen months, Lee had been exchanged and returned to duty only weeks before the pursuit of Clinton began. But in those weeks he did not like what he saw. The efforts to "Europeanize" the army appalled him; the Continentals, he said, would never beat the redcoats at their own game. If they tried, he warned, "they will make an Awkward Figure, be laugh'd at as a bad army by their Enemy, and defeated in every Recontre which depends on Manoeuvres."[35] Rather, he advised, the Americans should take advantage of terrain and the vastness of their country and fight a war of harassment and small unit operations—in effect, a guerrilla war. To men like Washington, Greene, and Wayne, who longed to trade volley for volley with the British and to assume the status and prerogatives traditionally associated with military rank in the eighteenth century, such ideas now seemed ridiculous and hopelessly out of step with the times. During his months of captivity, then, as John Shy has noted, "the war seemed to have moved beyond Charles Lee."[36]

At any rate, Lee spoke his mind on this occasion with his usual bluntness. He argued for letting Clinton go, in fact, for doing nothing to slow the British exit from New Jersey. Why risk the patriot regulars, he asked, in pointless action against the best-trained professional troops that Europe had to offer when prudence would accomplish results equally important? Would it not make more sense, he continued, to await the results of the active intervention of the French while conserving American strength? As it was, Lee stressed that a rebel victory would probably do the cause little good, while a defeat in a general action could do it irreparable harm.[37] And it should be noted that despite the unpopularity of Lee's views among many of the other officers and the pall cast over this able but eccentric man's career after Monmouth, his ideas had some solid merits. The French alliance and

the evacuation of Philadelphia had lifted patriot spirits to new heights and left the royal troops dejected and bitter. Clinton was looking for a chance—any chance—to redeem the honor of British arms, and a rash patriot attack could have played directly into his hands. So if Lee's conservative course would have brought no new laurels to the rebel army, neither would it have risked boosting British morale with even a partial victory over Washington.

Beset by the strongly held and conflicting opinions of his subordinates, Washington made a decision that pleased almost no one. Taking a middle ground (a position he had probably wanted to reach all along), he first agreed to reinforce further the advance corps already operating around Clinton. He accordingly ordered General Charles Scott and his fifteen hundred Virginians to the aid of Maxwell, Morgan and the militia.[38] This addition in strength brought the rebel vanguard to some thirty-five hundred regulars—a respectable force in the eyes of the twenty-year-old Lafayette, who happily took command after the disgruntled Lee had refused the assignment. Yet the more aggressive hawks, notably Hamilton and Greene, remained unsatisfied and even sought out their commander after the close of the council to plead the case for sending a still larger force against the British. Finally persuaded (either by his own reasoning or the supplications of his subordinates), Washington detached another thousand men under Anthony Wayne, who broke camp shortly after Scott's contingent.[39] But the commander in chief still was not looking for more than he could handle. He sent Lafayette a note on the 26th, again advising care. While hitting Clinton was "very desirable," he warned the Frenchman not to push his men too hard "by an over hasty march" in the hot weather, for fear that many of the men would "fall sick and be rendered entirely unfit for Service."[40] The Hopewell conference, then, had resulted in a sizeable movement toward the enemy, although it had hardly demonstrated Washington at his most decisive. The entire affair, a disgusted Hamilton noted acidly, "would have done honor to the most honorable society of midwives and them only."[41]

Yet Lafayette was overjoyed at his command, and he lost no time in taking out after Clinton. He in fact became downright rash. Planning to attack the royal battalions early on the 26th, he plunged ahead without adequate supplies for his troops, accurate intelligence of the British position, or even knowledge of the locations of all American formations. Worse, he advanced far beyond a point where Washington's main body could have supported him if, alone, he ran into trouble.[42] Washington heard of the marquis's movements with increasing apprehension; even the aggressive Hamilton, then serving as one of Lafayette's aides, saw a disaster in the making.[43] Finally, to the relief of almost everyone concerned, Lafayette called a halt with his troops exhausted and his supplies almost expended. Some of his outfits were already within a mile of Clinton's lines, so it had been a near thing. If a fight had developed, it is doubtful that the young general could have held his own. At this stage, a somewhat dismayed Washington reassumed the reins of command and ordered his disappointed subordinate to march his men to Englishtown (about eleven miles to the north), where Lafayette could resupply and the commander in chief could safely reassess the entire situation.[44]

The Chase Ends: Conflict at Freehold

While Lafayette moved toward Clinton, General Lee had second thoughts about refusing command of the advanced body. The addition of Wayne's men, as well as the presence of at least a thousand New Jersey militia, had made it a significant force. In fact, he wrote Washington, it was "undoubtedly the most honorable command next to" the commander in chief's; as the army's second-ranking officer, Lee now wanted it. It would look "odd," he noted, if a junior officer should lead such an important detachment, and a number of other senior generals concurred.[45] Washington could hardly deny the justice of the request, and he approved, with the provision that Lafayette be allowed to complete any operation already in progress.[46] Lee took command when Lafayette reached Englishtown on the afternoon of the 27th.

When Lee joined his troops, the American and British armies were on the eve of battle. Washington's main body now lay at Cranbury, about four miles west of the advanced corps at Englishtown. Dickinson's militia and Maxwell's Continentals, operating about three miles east of Englishtown, harassed Clinton's left flank. Daniel Morgan's riflemen, at Richmond's Mill, southeast of Freehold, harried Clinton's right flank.[47] Altogether, the rebel army had almost twelve thousand Continentals and well over a thousand militia in the field. Clinton, with an approximately equal number of men (including about three thousand provincials), was encamped along the road east and west of Freehold. He had stayed in town all day on the 27th, and it is likely that he was hoping for Washington to pick a fight. If so, he had little longer to wait.[48]

Lee's orders at this point were discretionary. That is, Washington had directed him to move against Clinton's rear on the morning of June 28, but Lee was to use his own judgment on exactly how and when to fight. And that included deciding whether to fight at all, as Lee was to desist if "there should be powerful reasons to the contrary."[49] Above all, the commander in chief emphasized that the advanced corps was not to get into a general engagement. Rather, Washington saw the projected attack, at least in its early stage, as a way to "harass" the enemy "as much as possible." Lee made it clear to his officers that he would act only within the confines of Washington's orders.[50] Still, he seemed in a fighting mood.

One wonders what was going through Lee's mind at this point. Was he smarting over differences with his more aggressive brother officers and looking for a chance to show them he could fight? Or, did he feel an obligation to erase the embarrassment of having first refused command of the vanguard? Or perhaps, because of Washington's order for a limited attack, had Lee thought that the senior general had moved toward his own less hawkish concept of operations? We have few clues on this, but it is sure that despite a lack of precise knowledge of the enemy's situation or of the terrain, he was determined to make the best showing possible.

Lee moved toward Freehold early on the 28th. Conflicting intelligence left the British positions obscure. But he knew from one of Dickinson's messages that Clinton's baggage was already moving toward Middletown. He was unable to determine the disposition of Clinton's main body. After a minor skirmish between a militia unit and a small party of dragoons, Lee halted before a causeway that spanned a ravine and creek outside of Freehold. He feared crossing because a retreat over the causeway in the face of a British attack would have been a dangerous proposition. In fact, General Dickinson, whom Lee met near the bridge, warned him pointedly that marching beyond the ravine would put the rebels "in a perilous situation" if Sir Henry stood and fought. After an hour's wait with no solid information on British movements, Lee's corps crossed the causeway, with Wayne's men in the lead.

Battle was joined at about 9:30 a.m. As Wayne moved on Freehold, his leading elements on the left (under Lieutenant Colonel Richard Butler) ran into the crack Queen's Rangers, commanded by Lieutenant Colonel John Graves Simcoe. The Rangers charged, and Butler's men sent them flying with a volley of musketry. Then the Americans spotted Lord Cornwallis's column marching out of town. Lee was convinced that this was only a strong rear guard and that by marching rapidly around Wayne's position on his left, he could circle in behind them and bag the lot. To occupy Cornwallis during this maneuver, Lee directed Wayne to pin down the enemy with a light fire. A full-scale attack would have driven the British back and made encirclement impossible. In theory the plan was a good one and, confident of success, Lee put his regiments in motion.

But from the beginning things went wrong. Lee's march across broken terrain was more difficult than anticipated. Wayne, expected only to "amuse" the British, apparently tried to hit them hard.[51] To Clinton, all this activity meant one of two things: either an attack on the British baggage train or a delaying tactic that would enable the rebels to beat him to Middletown and gain a favorable military position. He responded with an unsuccessful cavalry charge and then with artillery, which opened a noisy but largely harmless duel with patriot batteries.

But more important, he ordered Cornwallis to fall back toward Freehold, a maneuver which would counter the American attempt at encirclement. Lee saw the British move, but he was not alarmed. He still felt the engagement was under control.

At this point, however, Lee's battle plan fell apart. Cornwallis actually led six thousand of Clinton's best men. They rapidly closed on the American right and pushed Lafayette back. Meanwhile, Lee was infuriated to find that a major portion of his left had begun an unauthorized retreat. Orders had become confused, and some officers—who later claimed that Lee had never clearly explained his plans to them anyway—apparently mistook the movements of neighboring units for a general withdrawal. Fearful of being left behind as the British advanced on the right, they decided to pull out themselves. However the retreat started, Lee now saw that with battlefield communications collapsing and with Cornwallis coming on, there was no alternative but to withdraw. Livid with anger, he led a generally orderly retreat to another position, still on the Freehold side of the causeway they had crossed earlier. The new terrain proved indefensible and Lee decided to pull back to a better position beyond the causeway. The frustrated general withdrew across the causeway ahead of his troops, heading away from Freehold.

It was here that Lee met Washington, who had come up ahead of the main army. Bewildered and angered by the retreat, the commander in chief crossly interrupted Lee's attempt to explain the situation and personally took charge of events.[52] From then on, the American line rapidly stabilized. Cooling off, Washington put Lee back in charge of the front line where, perplexed by his superior's outburst, Lee performed creditably. Back on the Freehold side of the causeway, Lee fought a tough holding action while Washington organized another position on a rise on the far side of the bridge. For the rest of the day this new line held out against a series of grueling British assaults. Clinton pressed his attack, hoping that Washington was going to offer him an all-out fight.[53] But the Continentals, having regained their balance, fought doggedly and made several sallies across the causeway before darkness forced an end to the action.

It had been a tough fight. Combat was hand-to-hand at times, and acts of individual heroism occurred on both sides throughout the day. Not surprisingly, the casualty figures were high. Estimates of killed and wounded in both armies varied widely, but Clinton's losses were clearly more serious. He apparently had slightly over two hundred killed, with about as many wounded. American losses stood at about a hundred dead and one hundred sixty wounded. Among the dead, many were the victims of heat and exhaustion, as the armies had clashed in temperatures well over ninety degrees.[54]

Monmouth could have been a much larger battle. Washington had fought well in the afternoon; he had also fought conservatively. He made no effort to flank the British, and he seldom fought more than a few enemy detachments at a time. The engagement on the 28th was in no sense a general action. Washington, though, had hoped to resume the fighting on the morning of the 29th, but Clinton was having none of it. In Sir Henry's eyes, the British had fought a model rear-guard action and, although he did not get the major confrontation he sought, he at least saved his baggage train and assured the successful completion of his march. Satisfied with that he slipped away toward Middletown in the dark. Washington let him go. Shadowed by rebel parties, the British arrived at Sandy Hook two days later. On July 5 they sailed for New York and the Monmouth campaign was over.[55]

The Battle in Retrospect

In the technical sense the question of who won the battle of Monmouth is academic: both sides said they were happy with the results. The patriots (and many American historians since) pointed to Clinton's casualties and American possession of the field after the fight in claiming victory. Moreover, Washington was pleased to note that the fortunes of war had carried him back to the region from which he had rather ignobly retreated earlier in the war. "It is not a little pleasing," he wrote, "nor less wonderful to contemplate, that after two years of maneuvering and undergoing the strangest vicissitudes that perhaps attended any one contest since creation, both armies are brought back to the very point they set out from."[56] The British, in turn, ridiculed the American view of the affair and noted with some justification that under adverse conditions they had successfully marched through the whole of an enemy province—which was all they had wanted to do anyway. Clinton had not even lost a single wagon.[57] From strictly tactical perspectives, then, it is hard to disagree with Willard Wallace's observation that "if ever a battle was a drawn struggle, Monmouth was it."[58]

Much of the battle's significance, however, lay not in its tactical outcome, but in the things it demonstrated about the American war effort in general. In this regard, several points were salient. Perhaps the most obvious was the improved fighting capacities of the American regulars. Historians have traditionally noted that Monmouth marked a symbolic "coming of age" for the Continental Line—the first engagement in which their accumulated experience and training were clearly in evidence.[59] Although the rebel army still had serious weaknesses, notably in cavalry and field communications, the artillery and infantry had stood up well against some of the best troops in the world. Certainly most of the British officers credited the rebels with looking better than ever; and some of the American commanders, including junior officers, were absolutely exuberant over their showing. The army "gained Immortal honor," according to Major Joseph Bloomfield, as they resolutely faced "the flower of the British army, . . . the proud King's Guards and haughty British-Grenadiers."[60] Even Alexander Hamilton—formerly a fierce critic of the Continentals—was impressed: "You know my way of thinking about our army," he wrote to a friend after the battle, "and I am not about to flatter it. I assure you I never was pleased with them before this day."[61]

Beyond demonstrating the fighting abilities of the regulars, however, Monmouth also forced a resolution of another issue vital in the maturing of the rebel army. The entire matter of Lee's conduct during the action led to a final recognition, if one was even needed at this stage, of the sanctity of

Washington's position as commander in chief. After the fight, Lee had requested an apology for Washington's pointed words on the battlefield; and this being refused, he had demanded, in clearly insolent terms, a court martial to clear his name of rumored misconduct.[62] The military court charged him with disobeying Washington's orders to attack, with "making an unnecessary, disorderly, and shameful retreat," and with disrespect toward the commander in chief.

In a trial which most historians now concede did no credit to the army, Lee conducted a skillful and articulate defense. Given the circumstances of the battle, the first two charges against him were patently absurd.[63] He had undeniably been disrespectful to Washington, however, and "under the circumstances," as historian John Shy has observed, "an acquittal on the first two charges would have been a vote of no-confidence in Washington."[64] But after Monmouth, Washington's stock was never higher, and people no longer expressed, as some had in 1777, reservations about his ability. Given Lee's unpopularity among most of the officers, the verdict of guilty on all counts was not surprising. The court did, however, delete the word "shameful" from the second charge. Lee was suspended from the army for a year—a ridiculously light sentence if the court actually believed him guilty. When Congress sustained the judgment, Lee retired in disgust.[65]

I intend neither to judge Lee nor those who judged him. However, his removal eliminated Washington's last significant opposition within the officer corps. Neither Lee nor any other officer was a rival for Washington's position, but Lee's departure removed the last obstacle to Washington's goal of building a traditional regular army. When Lee left he took with him his conception of an American army based largely on a popular militia. And his fate served as an object lesson to those who would criticize the commanding general in the future.

But something more was clear in the American performance than just the improved status of the regulars. For if the Continentals had learned a lot in almost three years of war, so had patriot civilians and militiamen. There was evident in the Jersey countryside a pervasive hostility toward the British not present early in the Revolution. The invasion of 1776 and the raids in 1777, with the accompanying pillaging, had engendered a popular hatred of the king's troops. Clinton's reception in 1778 was considerably more hostile than Howe's in 1776. This time fewer Tories rallied to the Royal Army and intelligence was harder to gather. The Monmouth campaign clearly demonstrated that New Jersey was now hostile territory for the crown.

This intense popular attitude was nowhere more evident than in the conduct of the Jersey militia. Earlier in the war Washington had caustically denigrated it for a wretched performance, particularly in 1776. There were times in 1776 when the citizen-soldiers fled in the face of British advances, awed by the professional troops before them and terrified of Tory subversion around them.[66] By 1778, however, the picture had changed. While the militia still preferred not to face the redcoats in an open fight, at least the myth of British invincibility had been dispelled. The Loyalists were still dangerous, but by now most of them were known or had been forced to flee, lessening earlier militia fears of an organized counterrevolution. Moreover, after two years of war, state authorities—however haltingly—had improved the effectiveness of New Jersey's militia laws. Thousands of Jerseyans were carried on militia rosters and local officials began to compel service. Consequently, more militiamen began turning out for their tours of duty, and they gradually gained in experience and confidence. In 1778 the state's militia was not as effective as it would be two years later at the battle of Springfield. But it was clearly a force to be reckoned with. (We should note here, however, that thousands of eligible men still avoided militia service, and that even among those who served the duty was by no means popular.)[67]

The part-time soldiers, as demonstrated by the efforts of Dickinson's men, had learned well the arts of harassment, bushwhacking and intelligence gathering. Some of the militia also fought heroically in open battle beside the American regulars. At the end of the campaign, Washington, who knew the militia had contributed vitally to his ability to catch up to Clinton, was as liberal in his praise as he had been in his condemnation in 1776.[68] Clearly, if Monmouth showed the Continentals coming of age, it did the same for the militia.

Moreover, the ability of the Continentals and the militia to coordinate their activities effectively also deserves comment. As the social base of the Revolution broadened, the state militia drew more Jerseyans, however reluctantly, into active service. The increased effectiveness of the joint militia-Continental war effort became a visible sign of the revolutionary society. It showed most clearly how that society, embodied in the militia, could, once its activities were coordinated with those of the army, overwhelm and defeat an enemy.[69] The British had received a taste of this at Saratoga in 1777; Monmouth showed that the Americans could now repeat the performance.

These improvements in the rebel war effort—which I again emphasize went far beyond the increased efficiency of the Continentals—were matters of terrific importance when viewed in the broad military context of the Revolution. The Royal Army could still handle the relatively few crack Continental outfits, but to face a war-wise populace as well was another matter. Monmouth was one sign that this had become a problem for the British, and it was a problem they would never solve.

NOTES

1. On Howe's command in America see Ira D. Gruber, The Howe Brothers and the American Revolution (New York: Atheneum, 1972).
2. Quoted in William S. Stryker, The Battle of Monmouth, ed. William Starr Myers (Princeton: Princeton University Press, 1927), p. 33. Stryker's work, written from a local history perspective, is probably the best single source of information on the battle.
3. Don Higginbotham discusses the impact of the French entry into the war in The War of American Independence: Military Attitudes, Policies and Practice, 1763-1789 (New York: Macmillan, 1971), chap. 10. British military attitudes on giving up the city are noted in Theodore Thayer, The Making of a Scapegoat: Washington and Lee at Monmouth (Port Washington, N.Y.: Kennikat Press, 1976), pp. 25-26. Thayer's book is concise and accurate—the best brief overview of the battle available and, as the title implies, the famous Washington-Lee controversy.
4. Piers Mackesy, The War for America (Cambridge, Mass.: Harvard University Press, 1964), pp. 156-58, 252-56.
5. Thayer, Making of a Scapegoat, p. 25.
6. Quoted in ibid.
7. Stryker, Battle of Monmouth, pp. 28-29.
8. Ibid., pp. 22-23, 31-32.
9. Thayer, Making of a Scapegoat, p. 26.
10. George Washington to Horatio Gates, May 17, 1778, John C. Fitzpatrick, ed., The Writings of George Washington from the Original Manuscript Sources, 1745-1799, 39 vols. (Washington, D.C.: U.S. Government Printing Office, 1931-44), 11:401-3.
11. When Maxwell crossed the Delaware, he joined other New Jersey Continentals under Colonel Israel Shreve, who had been in the Burlington County region since March. They had been fairly busy combatting Tory activities, stopping illegal trade with the enemy in Philadelphia, and guarding the area against British raids. Shreve had already been supplying Washington with intelligence, and Washington's concern to establish the full New Jersey Brigade on the east bank of the Delaware indicated his worry over a possible enemy move in that direction. On the activities of the New Jersey Continentals before Clinton's evacuation, see the Journal of Joseph Bloomfield, May 1778, Lloyd W. Smith Collection, Morristown National Historical Park Library, Morristown, N.J.; Israel Shreve to Washington, March 28, 1778, George Washington Papers, 4th ser., Manuscripts Division, Library of Congress Washington, D.C.; Washington to Shreve, April 4, 1778, Fitzpatrick, Writings of Washington, 11:210; Shreve to Washington, April 9, 1778, Israel Shreve Papers, Special Collections Department, Alexander Library, Rutgers University New Brunswick, N.J.; John Shreve, "The Days of the Revolution," New Jersey Mirror and Burlington County Advertiser, December 29, 1853.
12. Washington to Henry Knox, May 17, 1778, Fitzpatrick, Writings of Washington, 11:407; Washington to Shreve, May 23, 1778, ibid., 11:436-43.
13. William Maxwell to Philemon Dickinson, June 6, 1778, Washington Papers; Dickinson to Washington, June 6, 1778, ibid.
14. Washington to Maxwell, May 29, 1778, Fitzpatrick, Writings of Washington, 11:479; Washington to Dickinson, May 24, 1778, ibid., 11:445-46, 468-69; Dickinson to Shreve, May 25, 1778, Shreve Papers, Dickinson to Washington, June 9, 1778, Washington Papers.
15. New-Jersey Gazette, May 27, 1778; Dickinson to Washington, June 15, 1778, Washington Papers; William Livingston to Washington, June 16, 1778, ibid.
16. Stryker, Battle of Monmouth, p. 42; Thayer, Making of a Scapegoat, p. 24.
17. On the state of the Continental Line after Valley Forge, see Willard M. Wallace, Appeal to Arms: A Military History of the American Revolution (1951; Chicago: Quadrangle, 1964), chap. 16. For contemporary comment on the improvement in the Continentals, see Joseph Reed to [Henry Laurens?], June 15, 1778, no. 888, Emmet Collections, New York Public Library, New York, N.Y., and John Patten to Thomas [?], May 15, 1778, no. 950, ibid. Marcus Cunliffe has provided a good view of Washington's hopes for the Continentals: see his "George Washington: George Washington's Generalship," in George Athan Billias, ed., George Washington's Generals (New York: William Morrow, 1964), pp. 3-21.
18. Stryker, Battle of Monmouth, p. 40.
19. Council of War, June 17, 1778, Fitzpatrick, Writings of Washington, 12:75-78; Stryker, Battle of Monmouth, pp. 57-58.
20. Washington's various orders at this time are reprinted in Stryker, Battle of Monmouth, pp. 59-64, 68-69.
21. Thayer, Making of a Scapegoat, p. 25.
22. Sir Henry Clinton to Lord George Germain, July 5, 1778, quoted in Stryker, Battle of Monmouth, p. 267.
23. Ibid., p. 268. The British had some idea who was to blame for their trouble, having identified Maxwell as one of their tormentors. See John Andre, Major Andre's Journal (New York: Arno Press, 1968), p. 75.

24. Ibid., p. 269; Thayer, Making of a Scapegoat, p. 27.
25. Washington to the President of Congress, June 28, 1778, Fitzpatrick, Writings of Washington, 12:128.
26. Thayer, Making of a Scapegoat, p. 26.
27. Bloomfield Journal, June 28, 1778, Smith Collection. Clinton called the Crosswicks action a "trifling skirmish" in his letter to Germain, July 5, 1778, quoted in Stryker, Battle of Monmouth, p. 268.
28. Ibid.
29. Thayer, Making of a Scapegoat, pp. 28-29.
30. At this point, Washington indicated that Maxwell and Dickinson were his main sources of information about the enemy. See the two letters of Washington to Dickinson, June 24, 1778, Fitzpatrick, Writings of Washington, 12:111-113; and Washington to Maxwell, June 24, 1778, ibid., 12:113-114.
31. Washington to Dickinson, June 24, 1778, ibid., 12:111-112; Council of War, June 24, 1778, ibid., 12:115-117.
32. Quoted in Thayer, Making of a Scapegoat, p. 30.
33. Quoted in Stryker, Battle of Monmouth, p. 77.
34. The best biography of Charles Lee is John Richard Alden's General Charles Lee: Traitor or Patriot? (Baton Rouge: Louisiana State University Press, 1951); for a penetrating short essay on this undoubtedly brilliant but eccentric man, see John W. Shy, "Charles Lee: The Soldier as Radical," in Billias, Washington's Generals, pp. 22-53.
35. Charles Lee, The Lee Papers, Collections of the New-York Historical Society . . . , 4 vols. (New York: 1872-75), 2:383-89.
36. Shy, "Charles Lee," p. 42.
37. Thayer, Making of a Scapegoat, p. 29.
38. Stryker, Battle of Monmouth, p. 78. Dave Richard Palmer, in his interesting The Way of the Fox: American Strategy in the War for America, 1775-1783 (Westport, Conn.: Greenwood Press, 1975), overstated his case when he concluded that Washington's cautious course was an indication that Lee had "carried the debate" at the council (p. 151). Washington, as we have seen, had been cautious from the beginning of the campaign.
39. Thayer, Making of a Scapegoat, p. 30.
40. Washington to the Marquis de Lafayette, June 26, 1778, Fitzpatrick, Writings of Washington, 12:121.
41. Quoted in Thayer, Making of a Scapegoat, p. 31.
42. Henry B. Carrington, Battles of the American Revolution 1775-1781 (New York: A.S. Barnes, 1877), pp. 414-15; Washington to Lafayette, June 26, 1778, Fitzpatrick, Writings of Washington, 12:122; Thayer, Making of a Scapegoat, p. 31-32.
43. Ibid., p. 32.
44. Howard H. Peckham has expressed a contrary view, that it was unfortunate for the Americans that Lafayette did not catch Clinton. See his essay, "Marquis de Lafayette: Eager Warrior," in Billias, Washington's Generals, pp. 212-38.
45. Quoted in Thayer, Making of a Scapegoat, p. 33.
46. Washington to Lee, June 26, 1778, Fitzpatrick, Writings of Washington, 12: 119; Washington to Lafayette, June 26, 1778, ibid., 12: 120; Thayer, Making of a Scapegoat, p. 33. For a fuller discussion of Lee's request for the command, see Stryker, Battle of Monmouth, pp. 100-3.
47. Maxwell to Washington, [June 25] 1778, Washington Papers; Dickinson to Washington, June 25, 1778, ibid.
48. Unless otherwise noted, the following battle narrative is based on Carrington, Battles of the Revolution, pp. 422-45; Samuel S. Smith, The Battle of Monmouth (Monmouth Beach, N.J.: Philip Freneau Press, 1964); and Stryker, Battle of Monmouth. A shorter, but useful treatment is Samuel S. Smith's The Battle of Monmouth, New Jersey's Revolutionary Experience, no. 25 (Trenton: New Jersey Historical Commission, 1975).
49. Quoted in Thayer, Making of a Scapegoat, p. 38. These words were not Washington's; they came from Lieutenant Colonel Richard Kidder Meade's testimony at Lee's court martial after the battle. Thayer's discussion of the nature of Washington's instructions to Lee—that the commanding general had left the ultimate decision to attack up to Lee—is the best treatment of the subject in the literature. See ibid., pp. 38-39.
50. Ibid., p. 37.
51. Wayne's conduct at this stage of the battle has been critized by Smith, who has called his action "inexcusable by normal military standards." Certainly Lee was not happy with the aggressive Pennsylvania general. See Smith, Battle of Monmouth (1975), p. 17.
52. Washington, contrary to popular myth, apparently did not swear at Lee, although he was undoubtedly upset with affairs as he found them. His exact words on the occasion are not known, but the issue has a literature all its own. Thayer provides a convenient resume of an argument historians have unnecessarily prolonged. See Making of a Scapegoat, pp. 52-53.
53. Clinton to Germain, July 5, 1778, quoted in Stryker, Battle of Monmouth, p. 268.
54. Ibid., p. 270; Howard H. Peckham, ed., The Toll of Independence: Engagement and Battle Casualties of the American Revolution (Chicago: University of Chicago Press, 1974), p. 52.
55. Thayer, Making of a Scapegoat, p. 68.
56. General Orders, June 30, 1778, Fitzpatrick, Writings of Washington, 12:131-32; quoted in Palmer, The Way of the Fox, p. 152.
57. Smith, Battle of Monmouth (1975), p. 24; Thayer, Making of a Scapegoat, p. 68.
58. Wallace, Appeal to Arms, p. 190.
59. See, for typical examples, Higginbotham, War of Independence, p. 247; Palmer, The Way of the Fox, p. 151; Thayer, Making of a Scapegoat, p. 64; John R. Alden, A History of the American Revolution (New York: Alfred A. Knopf, 1969), p. 392; James Thomas Flexner, Washington: The Indispensable Man (Boston: Little, Brown, 1969), p. 124.
60. Washington to the President of Congress, July 1, 1778, Fitzpatrick, Writings of Washington, 12:145; Thayer, Making of a Scapegoat, p. 64; Bloomfield Journal, Smith Collection.
61. Quoted in Thayer, Making of a Scapegoat, p. 64.
62. See the two letters of Washington to Lee, June 30, 1778, Fitzpatrick, Writings of Washington, 12:132-33.
63. The trial record makes fascinating reading; see Proceedings of a General Court-Martial . . . for the Trial of Major-General Lee (New York: privately reprinted, 1864).
64. Shy, "Charles Lee," p. 45.
65. Proceedings of a General Court-Martial . . . , pp. 238-39; Stryker, Battle of Monmouth, p. 246.
66. Mark E. Lender, The New Jersey Soldier, New Jersey's Revolutionary Experience, no. 5 (Trenton: New Jersey Historical Commission, 1975), p. 10; Flexner, Washington, pp. 84, 85, notes Washington's reactions to militia retreats in general.
67. On the New Jersey militia and its performance, see Mark Edward Lender, "The Enlisted Line: The Continental Soldiers of New Jersey" (Ph.D. diss., Rutgers University, 1975), pp. 25-56.
68. Washington to Dickinson, June 25, 1778, Fitzpatrick, Writings of Washington, 12:118.
69. This was one of the themes of John Shy's provocative essay, "The American Revolution: The Military Conflict Considered as a Revolutionary Conflict," in Essays on the American Revolution, ed. Stephen G. Kurtz and James H. Hutson (Chapel Hill: University of North Carolina Press, 1973), pp. 121-56.

HEROINES ALL:
THE PLIGHT OF WOMEN AT WAR
IN AMERICA, 1776-1778

Elizabeth Evans

It was customary in eighteenth-century Europe and America for women and children to accompany military ranks on marches and battlefields. In the French and Indian War (the struggle from 1754 to 1763 between France and Great Britain for American dominion), many wives, servants and mistresses of British troops participated in campaigns as did their colonial opposite numbers. During the Revolutionary War, large numbers of British women and children shared cramped quarters and scanty rations with families of German mercenaries on the voyage from England in troop or supply vessels. Military commanders did not favor women traveling with the army unless they were nurses and laundresses. They saw them as an encumbrance on the army because women consumed vitally needed food and could not properly care for their infants. In addition, German babies born in Britain and the colonies posed a naturalization problem. But officers would have insufficient recruits unless the army granted passage and rations for their families. Therefore, women were allotted half-rations, children quarter-rations. Authorities reasoned that allowing a quota of women and offspring would minimize troop desertions. But many German recruits intended to desert once in America and used the quota system to obtain free passage for their families.

The official quota of women attached to each regiment varied during the Revolution. In 1777 the British ratio was approximately one woman to every eight men; the German about one to thirty. Four years later, the ratio was one to four or five among the British and one to fifteen among the Germans. Marriages between soldiers and colonists accounted for the increase, as did the need for additional nurses, laundresses and cooks. The ratios are misleading, for they omit vast numbers of Loyalist refugees, servants, mistresses and prostitutes, who either obtained provisions for themselves or got them from the soldiers. Female rum sellers caused drunkenness among the rank and file who, pressed or bribed into service, sought relief from a war many detested.

Camp followers must have been a rugged and hardy lot to have endured the appalling hardships. When General John Burgoyne capitulated at Saratoga in 1777, hundreds of women and children with the British army were forced to march the two hundred miles to Cambridge and sleep on cold, wet earth en route. After watching them trek through the town, Hannah Winthrop wrote to her friend, Mercy Otis Warren:

I never had the least idea that the Creation produced such a sordid set of creatures in human figure—poor, dirty emaciated men, great numbers of women, who seemed to be the beasts of burden, having a bushel basket on their back, by which they were bent double; the contents seemed to be pots and kettles, various sorts of furniture, children peeping through gridirons and other utensils, some very young infants who were born on the road, the women bare feet, clothed in dirty rags.[1]

At Prospect Hill and Winter Hill the war prisoners were crammed into crude, partially open, makeshift huts, some holding as many as thirty or forty men, women and children. They slept in the cold on scanty straw; few had blankets. Officers' wives and mistresses fared better, riding in carriages and rooming in private homes. Among them were Fredericke von Riedesel (wife of a Hessian general), with her young children and servants; Lady Harriet Acland and Mrs. Henry Harmage (wives of British majors); and Anne Reynal, whose husband, Lieutenant Thomas Reynal, had been killed during the Saratoga campaign. It was common for each British regiment to have on its payroll six fictitious names (referred to as "warrant men"), part of whose pay was intended for the widows of regimental officers.

Prior to the conflict at Saratoga, Madame Riedesel, her children and servants, traveled for months in the army's midst, using a horse-drawn calash. Usually they had access to houses and inns along the route, but at one house they suffered an intense rebel cannonade; in other places, the abusive language of the citizenry. Once, during a bitterly cold and windy sleetstorm, they slept in the woods, among soldiers and the other camp followers.

Although the American army adopted the European tradition of having camp followers on commissary rolls, it never attempted to limit their numbers, though at times the men were without food. During the winter of 1777-78 at Valley Forge, the need for provisions was so critical that thousands of men, women and children perished. On rare occasions, high-ranking officers hired nurses, laundresses and cooks. Strict orders, however, prohibited the presence of prostitutes and mistresses; few of the men could have afforded them anyway. General George Washington issued orders berating women for disorderliness and asked that only those who were absolutely necessary be allowed to follow the army. But whenever an excess of women and children

was unavoidable, he insisted that extra rations be provided for them. The rebel government's superintendent of finance, Robert Morris, wanted to limit camp followers' rations to a fifteenth of that given to non-commissioned officers and privates. But the general wouldn't hear of denying women and children. During the last few months of the war he wrote to Morris, "I was obliged to give provisions to the extra women in these regiments or lose by desertion, perhaps to the enemy, some of the oldest and best soldiers in the service. The latter with too much justice remarked. 'Our wives could earn their rations, but the soldier, nay, the officer, for whom they wash has naught to pay them.' "[2] The general added that a reduction would particularly increase hardships in New York regiments, "which, in part, are composed of Long Islanders and others who fled with their families when the enemy obtained possession of those places and have no other means of subsistence. The cries of these women, the sufferings of their children, and the complaints of the husbands would admit of no alternative."[3]

Most American women who went on these expeditions did not do so for the sake of the revolutionary cause; the rebel states were more united in name than in anything else. Most of these women supported the army out of concern for the welfare of their own families. A few, such as Deborah Sampson, who served as a private in the Fourth Massachusetts Regiment, managed to pose as fighting men in the ranks. The vast majority, however, were refugees from enemy assaults on their homes or simply wished to help their half-clad, destitute, undernourished men. Women cooked the scanty rations, treated the ill and wounded, washed and mended tattered clothing, and foraged for provisions. They even plundered the enemy's dead and wounded. On October 7, 1777, the British lost the battle of Bemis Heights, the climactic action of the Saratoga campaign. That night, women from the American camp stripped enemy corpses of clothing and equipment.

In the spring of 1778 word reached Washington that the British and Hessians were preparing to evacuate Philadelphia. In the occupied town, Elizabeth Sandwith Drinker, wife of a Quaker merchant, penned in her diary on May 23: "The army, 'tis thought, is going in reality to leave us, to evacuate the city. Some hope 'tis not the case, though things look like it. Many of the inhabitants are going with them."[4] Over the next two days, she wrote that baggage belonging to British and Hessian officers was being placed aboard vessels, and that "a number of the citizens are in great distress on account of this movement of the British army."[5] Loyalists, from the lowest economic level to the highest, were hastily preparing to leave. Many feared that with a rebel seizure of Philadelphia, Parliament would acknowledge independence, and America would be lost. Many of these evacuating citizens would be among the nearly one-hundred thousand colonists who fled to Britain, the West Indies, Nova Scotia and other places in Canada before the war's end. Few were allowed or able to return.

One of the reasons for Loyalist opposition to the war was economic. Rebel occupation of Philadelphia would replace European hard currency with worthless American paper money. Loyalists feared a high rate of inflation and accompanying economic crisis. These fears proved well-founded. Those who remained in Philadelphia bartered in goods and used paper money only to pay taxes.

In addition, General Sir Henry Clinton's decision to leave the city made little political sense to the Loyalists in view of recent news from Britain. Just two months before, King George III had signed bills conciliatory to the rebels. One bill repealed oppressive taxation; the other appointed commissioners who were empowered to grant pardons, suspend any act of Parliament passed in reference to the colonies since February 10, 1763, and seek other means of quieting American disorders. Scores of Philadelphia's Loyalists had already petitioned Parliament to repeal oppressive tax measures.

Numerous families obtained passage on vessels sailing for New York and elsewhere. Others, less fortunate, clogged the roads and Delaware River barges, beginning a long and dangerous journey by carriage, wagon, or on foot, as refugees headed for New York with Clinton's army.

Mrs. Drinker's home overlooked the river, and on June 18 she wrote: "Last night it was said there was 9,000 of the British troops left in town, 11,000 in New Jersey. This morning when we arose there was not one redcoat to be seen in town. The encampment in New Jersey also vanished."[6]

In New Jersey, the throng of new refugees—the army would not feed them—joined the melange of troops' wives, children, mistresses and prostitutes, most of whom had been living under deplorable, squalid conditions. General Clinton, worried by the large influx of women and children, took disciplinary action at Haddonfield, ordering that camp followers on the quota list be segregated from those who were not and that all be kept from his troops. "The women of the army are constantly to march upon the flanks of the baggage of their respective corps," he commanded, "and the Provost Martial has received positive orders to drum out any woman who shall dare to disobey this order."[7] One woman who disobeyed the order was whipped and expelled from the camp. Clinton's column—troops, wagons and camp follower cavalcade—was twelve miles long and required strict regulations. Otherwise his men would have insufficient food and they would be ineffectual as a combat force.

With the elite First Division, commanded by Major General Charles, Lord Cornwallis, were approximately fifteen hundred wagons—the baggage and supply train—including laundry, bakery, and blacksmith shops on wheels. Behind these were carriages and wagons belonging to Philadelphians, with a multitude of other camp followers, all unprovided for. Clinton, aware that Washington's army desperately needed clothing, food and military equipment, feared an attack on his elite division. Therefore, he turned over the army's baggage and supply train to General Wilhelm von Knyphausen, Hessian commander of the Second Division. As a further precaution, he issued an order on the night of June 24 to have the Second Division march well ahead of the First. The New Jersey militia, under General Philemon Dickinson's command, destroyed bridges and blocked roads in the path of this forward division. Hundreds of Hessians burdened by uniforms and equipment either collapsed in the intense heat or deserted. Women and children continued on the march, though burned by the sun, drenched by occasional rains, assailed by mosquitoes, and fatigued by the monotony of travel and family routine. Sporadic skirmishes with rebel units infesting wooded areas were unsettling; children cried and women shouted obscenities as muskets spat bullets about them.

Women in both divisions joined the troops in pillaging houses and farms of friend and foe alike. Many of their victims, previously loyal to the crown, changed allegiance.

Washington intended to intercept Clinton's force, and he marched the Continental army from Valley Forge on the night of June 18-19. A number of camp followers were with the troops, though many fewer than accompanied the British. Wives of prominent officers did not join the expedition. Martha Washington, Catherine Greene (wife of General Nathanael Greene), Lady Stirling (wife of Major General William Alexander, Lord Stirling), and others had endured the winter months at the encampment, making shirts and mending uniforms, ministering to the ill, and dispensing food baskets to the needy. Historians have lauded their efforts, but have ignored the efforts of the wives of the common soldiers—badly clothed and undernourished women who suffered intolerably from illness and freezing weather. Historians have estimated that three thousand men died of starvation and disease at Valley Forge, but have failed to mention the many women and children who also perished there. The unsightly camp followers were severely criticized by men who favored ladylike demeanor and behavior. Doctor Albigence Waldo, a surgeon with the army, wrote contemptuously:

> What! though there are in rags, in crape,
> Some beings here in female shape,
> In whom may still be found some traces,
> Of former beauty in their faces,
> Yet now so far from being nice,
> They boast of every barefaced vice.
> Shame to their sex!'Tis not in these
> One ever beholds those charms that please.[8]

Nonetheless, these women courageously joined the march through New Jersey, forging through creeks and over rutted roads in drenching downpours and intense heat, and then fought beside the men.

Washington had mixed feelings about camp followers. He was compassionate about their plight, and he knew that many of his men would desert if their wives were not allowed to travel with them. Yet since he also realized that they obstructed troop movement, he commanded repeatedly throughout the war that women march behind the baggage. Attempting to regulate the camp followers, he issued the following order when the army left Valley Forge:

> The indulgence of suffering women to ride in wagons, having degenerated into a great abuse, and complaint having been made by the officers of the day that the plea of leave from officers is constantly urged when the wagon masters order such women down.
>
> It is expressly ordered that no officer grant such a leave for the future but the commanding officers of a brigade or the field officers of the day, who are to grant it only on account of inability to march, and in writing.[9]

Few of the women and children with the New Jersey regiments had been spared enemy depredations in their communities. In December 1776, about fourteen thousand British and Hessian troops were stationed in New Jersey, from Staten Island to Trenton and at towns along the Delaware River. They plundered and burned homes, farms, and fulling and grist mills. They butchered livestock, demolished orchards, confiscated horses and produce, and robbed stores. Soldiers spread the bloody flux (probably dysentery or cholera) and other distempers, smallpox, and venereal disease. In January 1777, Colonel George Measam wrote to General Anthony Wayne, then in Albany, that "the enemy make great devastation in their retreat, burning without distinction Tory's as well as Whig's houses. Great part of Princeton destroyed. Tory's as well as Whig's wives and daughters ravished and carried off with them."[10]

Ravish was a polite term for rape, and it occurred frequently in New Jersey. A newspaper correspondent reported atrocities:

> Besides the sixteen young women who had fled to the woods to avoid their brutality, and were there seized and carried off, one man had the cruel mortification to have his wife and only daughter (a child of ten years of age) ravished; this he himself, almost choked with grief, uttered in lamentations to his friend, who told me of it, and also informed me that another girl of thirteen years of age was taken from her father's

house, carried to a barn about a mile, there ravished, and afterwards made use of by five more of these brutes. Numbers of instances of the same kind of behaviour I am assured of have happened . . . . Another instance of their brutality happened near Woodbridge; one of the most respectable gentlemen in that part of the country was alarmed by the cries and shrieks of a most lovely daughter; he found an officer, a British officer, in the act of ravishing her.[11]

An officer of the Continental army described a rape by British dragoons at Penns Neck, about two miles from Princeton. Two men

pretended to a young woman that they was searching for rebels, and had been informed that some of them were secreted in the barn and desired her to go with them and show them the most secret places there . . . She (knowing that nobody was there), to convince them, went to the barn with them to show them that nobody was there . . . When they had got her there, one of them laid hold on her, strangled her to prevent her crying out, while the other villain ravished her . . . When he had done, he strangled her again while the other brute repeated the horrid crime upon her again. She is a farmer's daughter, but her name, with her father's must be kept secret to avoid . . . reproach.[12]

Such savages were rarely, if ever, court-martialed.

In contrast, George Washington issued strict orders forbidding the plundering of any persons and saw that they were carried out. In June 1780 Thomas Brown (Newark soldier of the Second New Jersey Regiment) was court-martialed for desertion, sentenced to death, but was pardoned by Washington. The following month, Brown (then in the Seventh Pennsylvania Regiment) was again tried, this time for having plundered inhabitants of Paramus, where he molested a woman. He was hanged.

Before daybreak on June 28, 1778, General von Knyphausen's Second Division left Monmouth Court House (Freehold), in Monmouth County. Hours later the First Division followed. The army left in its wake many dead cattle and household furniture hacked in pieces, all owned by the town's inhabitants, most of whom had fled with the possessions they could carry. General Clinton had established his headquarters in the home of elderly Elizabeth Covenhoven, who

had to sleep on her cellar door in the milk room. As noon approached on June 28, Major General Charles Lee's American contingent was close to the town; Washington's main body of troops was about five miles behind. Lee's advanced corps attacked the enemy's rear guard about a mile or two northeast of the courthouse. The British responded with heavy fire. Both troops and camp followers cursed Lee's subsequent retreat. When Washington's main force intervened and strengthened American resistence, they cheered.

The day-long battle raged under a scorching sun, in nearly hundred-degree heat. One segment of the American force, a mixture of troops and camp followers, faced a British contingent of about two thousand. While British artillery fire exploded in their midst, American women helped the troops by aiding the wounded, firing muskets and assisting artillerymen.

They faced the hated, green-coated Queen's Rangers, whose many New York and Connecticut Loyalists had terrorized Americans on the outskirts of Valley Forge the winter before with will-o'-the-wisp guerrilla tactics. They fought wave after wave of scarlet-coated "lobsterbacks," blue-uniformed British artillerymen and Hessian grenadiers, and green-clad Jaegers.

Women were in the enemy's midst, a common sight during battles. In the early 1790s, when the duke of York undertook an expedition to Holland, an officer or soldier serving in the earl of Moira's force wrote of women's courage:

It would be doing great injustice to the women of the army not to mention with what alacrity they contributed all the assistance in their power to the soldiers while engaged, some fetching their aprons full of cartridges from the ammunition wagons, and filling the pouches of the soldiers, at the hazard of their own lives, while others with a canteen filled with spirit and water, would hold it to the mouths of soldiers, half choked with gunpowder and thirst, and when a man was wounded they would afford him all the assistance in their power to help him to the nearest house or wagon, in which friendly offices it was, as may be supposed, no uncommon thing for the females to get wounded as well as the men, many instances of the kind happening in the course of the campaign.[13]

When Washington intervened at Freehold, his first concern was to keep the enemy from flanking the army. He ordered General Greene to position his artillery on the right at Combs Hill, and Lord Stirling, commanding the left wing, to place his battery overlooking the west ravine. An intense artillery duel between the Continentals and the British lasted about two and a half hours. British troops attacked Stirling's force, but they were rebuffed by enfilading fire.

During the heat of the firing that sweltering Sunday afternoon, a strong young Irishwoman, coarse in speech, supplied her husband and others under Stirling's command, with containers of water drawn from a nearby farm well. Her Irish husband, William Hays, was a gunner in Captain Francis Proctor's Fourth Company of the Pennsylvania State Regiment of Artillery, commanded by Colonel Thomas Proctor. Hays and his wife Mary, nicknamed Molly, had fought Knyphausen's troops at the Brandywine in September, when the Americans were forced to retreat. She knew how to load and fire both musket and cannon.

During the battle of Monmouth, Joseph Plumb Martin, a private fighting with the Eighth Connecticut Regiment, also under Stirling's command, took a moment to observe Mary Hays.

> A woman whose husband belonged to the artillery . . . attended with her husband at the piece the whole time. While in the act of reaching a cartridge and having one of her feet as far before the other as she could step, a cannon shot from the enemy passed directly between her legs without doing any other damage than carrying away all the lower part of her petticoat. Looking at it with apparent unconcern, she observed that it was lucky it did not pass a little higher, for in that case it might have carried away something else, and continued her occupation.[14]

This implies that she had picked up a cartridge box at some point and was preparing to load and fire a musket, probably at the time when Stirling's force was under attack by the Queen's Rangers and the British light infantry.

Doctor Albigence Waldo, then with General Jedediah Huntington's Connecticut Brigade, treated a wounded officer who told him: "One of the camp women I must give a little praise to. Her gallant, whom she attended in battle, being shot down, she immediately took up his gun and cartridges and like a Spartan heroine fought with astonishing bravery, discharging the piece with as much regularity as any soldier present."[15] The woman may or may not have been Mary Hays. If so, the wounded man whose musket she retrieved was not William Hays, but a fallen comrade.

Mary Hays, or "Molly Pitcher," as she was later called, and Margaret Corbin, who fired a cannon during the fight for Fort Washington in 1776 (though her body was torn by grapeshot), should be remembered, not for their courage alone, but for all the women who participated in campaigns.

NOTES

1. Warren-Adams Letters . . . , Collections of the Massachusetts Historical Society, 2 vols. (Boston: 1917-25), 2:451-52.
   Eds. note. Capitalization, punctuation and spelling in this and all subsequent quotations in this paper have been modernized.
2. John C. Fitzpatrick, ed., The Writings of George Washington from the Original Manuscript Sources, 1745-1799, 39 vols. (Washington, D.C.: U.S. Government Printing Office, 1931-44), 26:78-80.
3. Ibid.
4. Elizabeth Sandwith Drinker Diary, Historical Society of Pennsylvania, Philadelphia, Pa.
5. Ibid.
6. Ibid.
7. Stephen Kemble, The Kemble Papers, Collections of the New-York Historical Society . . . , 2 vols. (New York: 1884-85), 1:595.
8. Albigence Waldo, "Valley Forge," Historical Magazine, 7 (September 1863): 270-74.
9. Fitzpatrick, Writings of Washington, 12:94.
10. George Measam to Anthony Wayne, January 11, 1777, Bancroft Transcripts, Anthony Wayne Letters, New York Public Library, New York, N.Y.
11. William S. Stryker, Archives of the State of New Jersey: Documents Relating to the Revolutionary History of the State of New Jersey, 2d ser., 5 vols.; vol. 1, Extracts from American Newspapers, 1776-1777 (Trenton: John L. Murphy 1901): 245-46.
12. Varnum Lansing Collins, ed., A Brief Narrative of the Ravages of the British and Hessians at Princeton in 1776-77 (1906; New York: Arno Press, 1968), p. 15.
13. Cecil C.P. Lawson, A History of the Uniforms of the British Army, 3 vols., (London: Norman Military Publications, Ltd., 1961-63), 3:107.
14. Joseph Plumb Martin, Private Yankee Doodle. Being a Narrative of Some of the Adventures, Dangers and Sufferings of a Revolutionary Soldier, ed. George F. Scheer (Boston: Little, Brown, 1962), pp. 132-33.
15. William S. Stryker, The Battle of Monmouth, ed. William Starr Myers (Princeton: Princeton University Press, 1927), p. 189.

COMMENTS

James Kirby Martin

Nearly two months ago, in mid-February 1978, I took my family to Valley Forge for a vacation weekend. It was a miniretreat from the confusing pace of our own times, representing, in theory, an opportunity to get my mind away from contemporary issues and back to those of the eighteenth century, the time frame in which a scholar of early American history should naturally want to focus his thoughts. We stayed two days and nights; the weather—cold, snowy, and windy—was perfect for evoking proper moods. It was the weekend of Washington's birthday; living history groups were camped out on those rolling hills, adding further to the authenticity of that scene of what it must have been like to have been with the Continental army, to have lived, suffered, and perhaps even died while in company with that virtuous and committed band of beleaguered men and women.

My point in relating this personal anecdote is that it is always difficult to recapture the essence of the past. At best, historians must acknowledge the distorting prism of time when attempting to cope with incidents and events, with people, their lives, and their values in ages long since buried. Yet we must continually challenge Clio and her veiled secrets with an eye to new insight, our objective being as much to understand our own times and ourselves (in proper historical perspective) as to gain a

sense of the din and clamor of human interactions now dimmed in memory by the inexorable passage of time.

With this preface in mind, let me turn to the papers. Professor Lender has done a job as exacting as that of any other author who has taken us back to Monmouth Court House. We have seen the simmering tension that turned into an explosion between Charles Lee and George Washington. We have felt the bitterly hot and muggy weather, perhaps causing as many casualties from heat exhaustion as from the convulsions of the battle itself. Even more important, we have looked at the event in a broadened time frame, stretching from Valley Forge to Clinton's final retreat to Sandy Hook and New York. And Dr. Lender has outlined some of the most salient points of significance surrounding the Monmouth clash, including the unassailability of Washington's position as commander in chief, the growing sophistication of irregular militia units, and the reorganized vigor of the Continental soldiery, now trained so much better by the likes of Friedrich von Steuben at Valley Forge.

Let me state the matter somewhat differently. This is a paper rich in the tradition of commentary about Monmouth. It compares favorably with the work of William S. Stryker, Samuel S. Smith, and Theodore Thayer.[1] In fact, I would argue that it is the best overview of the battle that has been written to date.

Having concluded that, I must also point out that Dr. Lender's paper is bounded by the confines of rather traditional questions about the Monmouth clash, questions such as Washington or Lee, good or bad, right or wrong; the militia, a help or a hindrance; the American army, better-trained but perhaps not really ready for the larger task at hand. Finally, who won the battle? Too often, it can be asserted, Monmouth has been viewed from a traditional "guns, battles, and tactics" perspective—which may not be the most revealing basis for comprehending what was really going on, particularly with respect to Monmouth as an element in the whole chemistry of the American War for Independence.

I would like to suggest that a different mix of elements, dwelling more on the British side of things, will prove to be more revealing, especially when we combine that mix with an assessment of American problems. It would be in poor taste to offer a detailed analysis here, as that would involve a separate paper rather than brief comments. But let me place before you a formula for what might be included in such a presentation.

We must begin by raising two basic questions: Why did the Americans win the war? Why did the British lose? Then we would lay a somewhat controversial hypothesis on the table by asserting that, given the times, it should have been virtually impossible for Great Britain to have won the war, or for the Americans to have lost it. The disadvantages facing Great Britain in 1775 were staggering. They can be summarized by arguing that trying to reconquer by martial force what had been lost through a breakdown in political communications and human understanding was a nearly impossible military task. The fact that Great Britain's armed forces, no doubt among the most powerful and well-trained in the world at that time, were in no way capable of conquering the eastern edge of a vast continent through accepted military strategies and tactics made the assignment even more difficult. Moreover, the technology was not there. Not only were standing European armies small, but their firepower was diffuse

and weak: the weapons during this age of limited war were often ineffective unless bayonets glistened in hand-to-hand combat. Military thinking emphasized concentration of forces, striking at vital points on the map. But how could the British concentrate troops on a strategically vital point in America when even the capture of Philadelphia during the autumn of 1777 had no particular impact on rebel behavior? From the outset, the reality of the war was that the erstwhile colonies, large and diverse geographically, represented a virtually impossible target for conquest by small-scale regular armies and navies of the standard eighteenth-century type.

In this framework, then, it seems strange that the British had done so well, relatively speaking, in the War for American Independence before 1778—and the Americans so poorly. But had that been the case? Great Britain had committed just about everything in sight to the campaign effort of 1776, concentrating on New York. But everything had not been enough. The 1777 British campaign effort was one more step downhill and was followed by the lost opportunity of the Monmouth campaign. Formal French intervention in the late winter of 1777-78 was the final intolerable strain for the British military lion. The rebellion was turning into a world war. Land and naval forces would have to be dispersed to other parts of the globe to cope with the awakened French adversary.

Indeed, Sir Henry Clinton, in June 1778, retreated from Philadelphia to New York under direct orders from the home government. Clinton's army was to be dispersed to meet new challenges on new fronts. A large military force, drawn partly from his army, was to be sent to the West Indies. And the British military establishment, no longer able to focus its efforts on specific American targets, would have to change its strategy to have any chance of victory. Given the state of eighteenth-century weaponry and the British inability to concentrate their forces, reconquering the continent became an all-but-hopeless task.

By the early summer of 1778 the principal question had become: Could the Americans sustain their rebellion, given the overwhelming obstacles that now faced the British? At Monmouth, the Continentals provided an answer: an equivocal yes. If the rebels could recover the commitment and public virtue of 1776, victory might be theirs.

Irony, as much as the agony of the weather and the scorching of human flesh, infused the battle of Monmouth. Victory should have been there all along, but the grand prize eluded the Americans for a few more years. An assessment of Britain's perspective and its real military difficulties provides a broader framework for understanding the significance of the battle.[2]

Turning to Elizabeth Evans's presentation, we must consider a different set of issues. While Dr. Lender, even with his traditional focus, has offered us new insight and solid interpretation, Ms. Evans's paper may best be described as a descriptive compilation that does not do much to refine and deepen our knowledge of women in the revolutionary era. For those who think that this may be an excessive statement, I would ask you to consider the recent writings of Carol Berkin, Linda Grant De Pauw, Linda Kerber, and Mary Beth Norton, among others.[3]

Ms. Evans's paper consists of three overlapping sections: (1) women in the two armies; (2) selected examples of atrocities against women; and (3) a passing glance at Molly Pitcher and the battle of Monmouth. Apparently, we should be surprised to learn that women traveled with both armies, that some of them were "on the ration"; that they most often specialized in critical support functions and a few, like the prototypical Molly Pitcher, were swept into the tide of battle. This is hardly news to students of eighteenth-century military history (especially those familiar with the American Revolution). But what does all this mean? If Evans had asked that question, we would have a very important paper on our hands. Since she did not, I will offer some tentative analytical comments, especially about the women of the Continental army.

Walter H. Blumenthal's Women Camp Followers of the American Revolution (1952; New York: Arno Press, 1974) is a reasonable starting point. Like Evans, Blumenthal suggests that those American women in the ranks were there out of concern for their families and communities. The implication is that these women, unlike British camp followers, came from all classes of society. Most were the wives of Washingon's embattled farmers, supporting their husbands in the cause of liberty—as epitomized by the legendary Molly pitcher.

Unfortunately for the myth, recent historical research has largely undermined the embattled-farmer tradition. Detailed quantitative investigations of the social composition of the Massachusetts, New Jersey, Maryland, and Virginia lines have demonstrated that Continental regulars, after the initial war enthusiasm of 1775 faded, were everything but middle-class freeholders and artisans. Washington's men were down-and-outers. As a group, they were very poor. Many were not free; military service was a welcome alternative to prison, indentured servitude, or chattel slavery. The freeholders who were the citizen soldiers of the myth were, in reality, part-time soldiers who served in the militia. The Continental regulars, largely society's downtrodden, saw the war as a chance to earn their personal freedom and economic self-respect.[4]

The army's social composition was probably duplicated among the women in the ranks. There were no Abigail Adamses or Mercy Otis Warrens "on the ration" or trailing along behind the army. When the "better sort" of women were in camp, they were invariably visiting their officer husbands. Women of the status of Martha Washington, Catherine Greene, and Lady Stirling would never have been permitted near a battle, much less to scavenge a battlefield or bury corpses (both standard duties for women in the ranks). Most of the women were young, single, and poor, as were most of the men.[5]

Why would these women associate with the army? First, some did follow their husbands, most commonly when such family units lacked property to sustain themselves. Second, some were prostitutes. Third, and most important, many were single and in desperate need of the bare necessities of life. The army offered half rations, clothing and other goods that came with regular military service. In return for their rations these women performed support functions, both domestic and military.

One can assert that these women fought not only for political freedom, but also for their own social, economic, and cultural

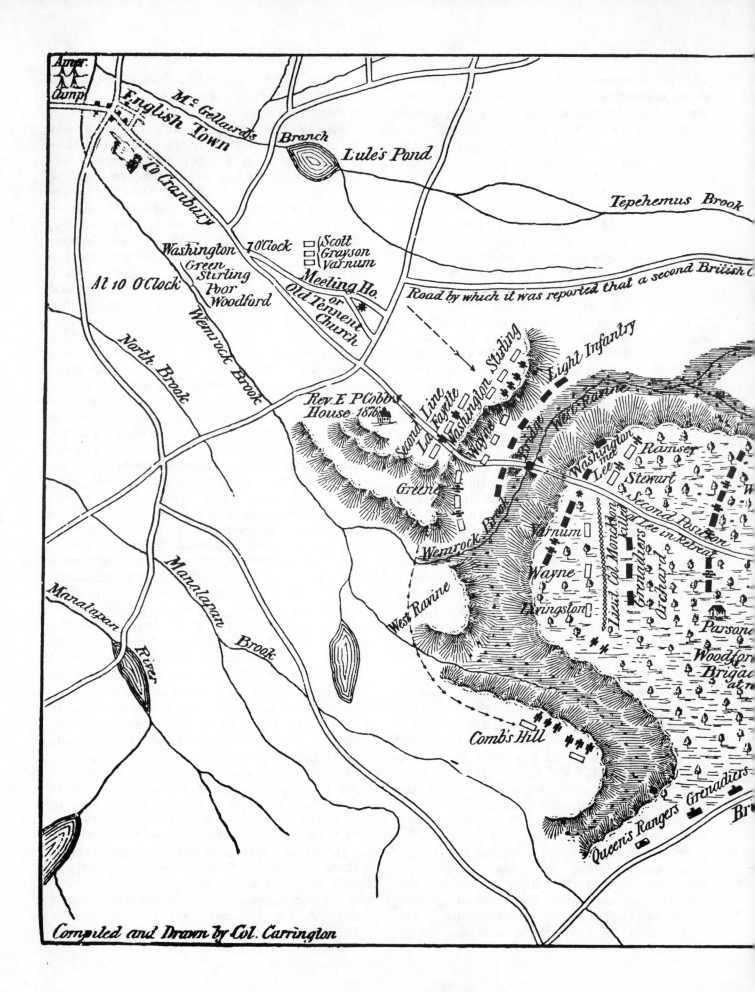

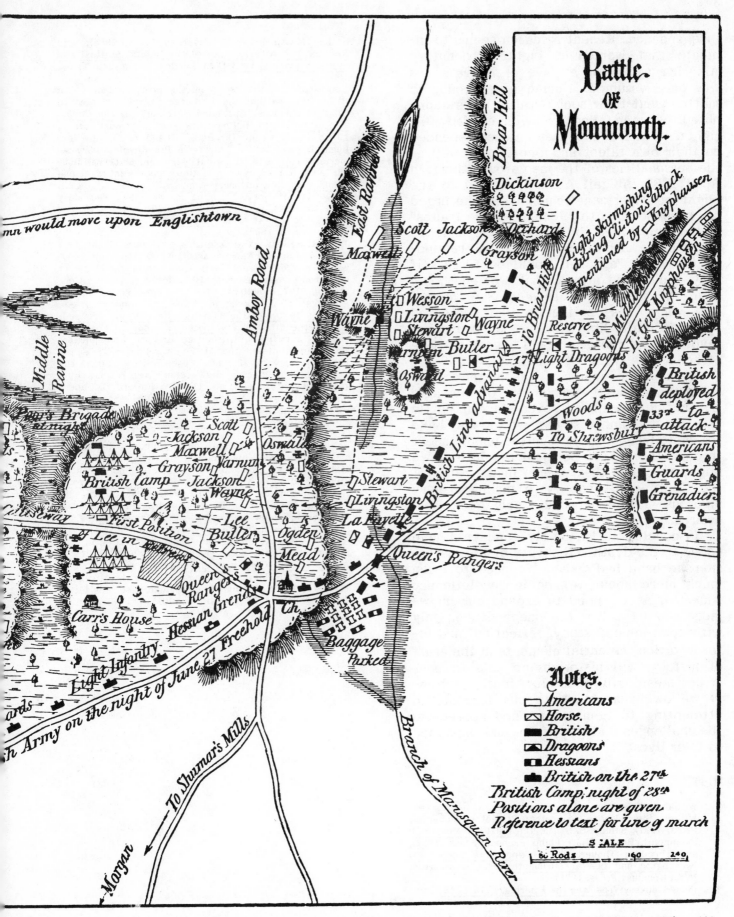

From Henry B. Carrington, Battles of the American Revolution (New York: A.S. Barnes, 1876), p. 444.

independence. Recent research seems to indicate that women in eighteenth-century America were not as free or liberated as was once assumed. Women as a group, no matter what their social status, were dominated by men. Legally, women had few rights. What freedom they enjoyed depended on their own talent and ambition as well as the personalities of the men around them. In April 1776, Abigail Adams referred to the plight of American women when she urged her husband John to "Remember the Ladies" as he campaigned for national independence in the name of political liberty. She reminded him that "all Men would be tyrants if they could" and argued that women should have the same rights as men. She thought that women were neither free nor protected by fundamental liberties. She hoped that the revolutionary rhetoric would have a positive effect on the status of women.[6]

Perhaps the women of Washington's army were conveying the same sort of message: Let us fight for liberty, even stand in battle and fire the cannon so that we too may have the same freedom that a united people seeks through the act of political revolution. We might conclude, that women in the ranks of the Continental army were making a very vigorous statement about their needs and desires.

In conclusion, I hope my comments have added to the depth and quality of the discussion we have had today. We need to learn much more about women in revolutionary America, as we need to expand our knowledge about the War for Independence. Only with open-minded study, reflection, and interpretation, essential elements in the craft of history, will historians be able to construct meaningful generalizations. Certainly we owe that much to our forbears in attempting to comprehend and appreciate the challenges that gave form and substance to their lives.

NOTES

1. William S. Stryker, The Battle of Monmouth, ed. William Starr Myers (Princeton: Princeton University Press, 1927); Samuel S. Smith, The Battle of Monmouth (Monmouth Beach, N.J.: Philip Freneau Press, 1964); and Theodore Thayer, The Making of a Scapegoat: Washington and Lee at Monmouth (Port Washington, N.Y.: Kennikat Press, 1976).
2. Piers Mackesy, The War for America, 1775-1783 (Cambridge, Mass.: Harvard University Press, 1964); Eric Robson, The American Revolution in its Political and Military Aspects, 1763-1783 (London: Batchworth Press, 1955).
3. Representative writings from this group include Carol R. Berkin, "Within the Conjurer's Circle: Women in Colonial America," in Thomas Frazier, ed. The Underside of American History (New York: Harcourt, Brace, 1978); Linda Grant De Pauw, "Land of the Unfree: Legal Limitations on Liberty in Pre-Revolutionary America," Maryland Historical Magazine, 68 (1973): 355-68; Linda Kerber, Women of the Republic: Intellect and Ideology in Revolutionary America (Chapel Hill, N.C.: University of North Carolina Press, 1980); and Mary Beth Norton, Liberty's Daughters: The Revolutionary Experience of American Women, 1750-1800 (Boston: Little, Brown, 1980).
4. John R. Sellers, "The Origins and Careers of the New England Soldier: Noncommissioned Officers and Privates in the Massachusetts Continental Line" (paper delivered at the American Historical Association Convention, 1972); Sellers, "The Common Soldier in the American Revolution," in Stanley J. Underdal, ed., Military History of the American Revolution: Proceedings of the 6th Military History Symposium (Washington, D.C.: Office of Air Force History, Headquarters USAF; and United States Air Force Academy, 1976), pp. 151-161; Mark E. Lender, "The Enlisted Line: The Continental Soldiers of New Jersey" (Ph.D. diss. Rutgers University, 1975), pp. 110-139; Edward C. Papenfuse and Gregory A. Stiverson, "General Smallwood's Recruits: The Peacetime Career of the Revolutionary War Private," William and Mary Quarterly, 3rd Ser., 30 (1973): 117-132.
5. For discussions of the position of women in the Continental army, see John Todd White, "The Truth About Molly Pitcher," in James Kirby Martin and Karen R. Stubaus, ed., The American Revolution: Whose Revolution? (Huntington, N.Y.: R.E. Krieger, 1977), pp. 99-105, and Linda Grant De Pauw, "Women in Combat: The Revolutionary War Experience," Armed Forces and Society, 7 (1981): 209-26.
6. Abigail Adams to John Adams, March 31, 1776, in L.H. Butterfield et al., eds., The Adams Papers, Series 2, Adams Family Correspondence, 4 vols. to date (Cambridge, Mass: Harvard University Press, 1963- 1973), 1:369-71; for the reply of John Adams, see his letter dated April 14, 1776, contained in ibid., pp. 381-83.

LEE BEFORE MONMOUTH: A REAPPRAISAL OF HIS MILITARY CAREER

Dennis P. Ryan

As a documentary editor and a sometime military historian I feel I can bring a fresh eye to the life and times of Charles Lee before his participation in the battle of Monmouth. To this end, I can reexamine his personal life and military career and help fashion a new appraisal that assesses his achievements, shortcomings and failures.[1] Extensive extracts from Lee's correspondence may measure the man better through his own words than through the prism of his friends and enemies.

Charles Lee was born in Chester, England, on January 26, 1732. His father was a colonel in the Forty-fifth Regiment, and his mother was descended from the Burnbury family which was active in British politics.[2] In the absence of documents, little is known about Lee's early life. Although he came from a family of seven children, the deaths of all of his brothers gave him the undivided attention of his father, who inured him to military training. Lee was commissioned an ensign in his father's regiment when he was only fourteen. The commission actually preceded his formal education at Bury St. Edmunds in Suffolk. His father's death in 1750 placed Lee under his mother's financial domination until her death. Here again, in the absence of letters of the period, the psychological interplay of independent mother and dependent son offers the psychohistorian the opportunity only for spec-

ulation.[3] There is no doubt of Lee's deep affection for his sister, Sidney, who became his constant correspondent.

On May 1, 1751, Charles Lee was promoted to lieutenant in the Forty-fourth Regiment, after having been stationed in Ireland since 1748. Despite the lack of material on his formal education, we know that he used the months and years of peacetime duty to become a wide-ranging reader in the classics. In 1755 Lee's regiment embarked for America and service with Major General Edward Braddock in the French and Indian War. Lee fought in the Virginia campaign and was present for Braddock's defeat at the battle of the Wilderness near Fort Duquesne (modern Pittsburgh). His regiment wintered near Albany, New York. In his earliest surviving letter from America Lee wrote in admiration of Philadelphia society and the vast breadth of frontier New York. He became friendly with the Mohawk Indians and confessed to having married a daughter of a Seneca chief. The letter reveals a romantic attitude and a scholarly inquisitiveness common to many contemporary Anglo-Americans.[4]

At this stage of his military career the appropriateness of Lee's Indian name "Boiling Water," was becoming apparent. Given his low rank, Lee exhibited none of the discretion appropriate to an aspiring young officer. In a letter to his sister he labeled his former commander, Major General James Abercromby, "a damn'd beastly poltroon (who to the scourge and dishonour of the Nation, is unhappily at the head of our Army, as an instrument of divine vengeance to bring about national losses and national dishonor)."[5] In the letter he enclosed a narrative of the disastrous campaign to capture Fort Ticonderoga in the summer of 1757. He directed that it be given to a fellow officer and others who wished to read of "an eye witness to such superlative blundering, pusillanimity, and infamy."[6] Lee's intemperate behavior and his criticism of a superior without the cloak of confidentiality became one of his serious flaws. Two other incidents that illustrate his willingness to vent his feelings regardless of the consequences were an altercation with a major in his regiment and a legal controversy over recruiting an apprentice.

With the surrender of Montreal in 1760 the British had conquered Canada, and Charles Lee sailed for home. A man of twenty-eight, Lee had already shown the traits that would characterize him thirteen years later on his return to the colonies. On his return to England Lee showed little restraint, continuing to write with alarming candor. He wrote an anonymous pamphlet advising the ministry to keep Canada as a British colony after the hostilities with France had concluded. Political pressure finally brought him a promotion to major on August 10, 1762. To add to his military experience, he joined a British expeditionary force to aid the Portuguese against Spain in 1762. While he was serving under General John Burgoyne, his spirited action in charge of English cavalry and grenadiers near Villa Velha won him a field colonelcy in the Portuguese army as a reward for his bravery.

On his return to England Lee experienced the problems of seeking promotion in a peacetime army. Although King George III had indirectly promised him a promotion, Lee was retired from active service against his will in November 1763.[7] We can only speculate on the reasons for this treatment; one biographer suggests that his superiors resented Lee's intemperate statements.[8] A man of great energy, he quickly steered his career around this obstacle by seeking his

fortune in Poland. He managed to secure a recommendation from the son of a former friend of the Polish king Stanislas II Poniatowski, who had recently come to the throne through the machinations of the Russian empress, Catherine II. Before he sailed in December 1764, Lee described his feelings to Sir Charles Burnbury: "My present scheme is this, to go into the Polish service, to which I am so strongly recommended that I can scarcely fail. What can I do better? I see no chance of being provided for at home; my income is miserably scanty; my inclinations greater than those who are ignorant of my circumstances suppose."[9]

The intrigues and nuances of courting favor among nobility became a major part of Lee's life for several years. He skillfully used his knowledge of America to gain the ear of the Polish king and of King Frederick II of Prussia. King Stanislas appointed the young Briton his personal aide-de-camp. Although he professed that he and the king were ideologically united by liberal sentiments, Lee's views of Poland and its common citizens were far from democratic: "Were I to call the common people brutes, I should injure the quadruped creation, they are such mere moving clods of stinking earth."[10] After a brief diversion to Constantinople he received word of his mother's death and returned to England.

Great Britain in late 1766 differed notably from the political milieu Lee had left in 1764. The Stamp Act (March 22, 1765) had produced a heated debate in Britain and America about individual liberty, constitutional rights and the power of Britain to tax her colonists. Parliament repealed the act on March 18, 1766, but at the same time passed the Declaratory Act, reaffirming its authority over the colonies. Lee's letters from Poland to his English friends give early evidence of his Whig belief that unrestricted monarchy gravely threatened a constitutional arrangement between the people's representatives and their king. On March 1, 1766, he wrote to Sidney of his support for American resistance: "May God prosper the Americans in their resolutions, that there may be one Asylum at least on the earth for men, who prefer their natural rights to the fantastical prerogative of a foolish perverted head because it wears a Crown."[11] Such comments, more radical than the vociferous cries of the Sons of Liberty, suggest the personal animus that Lee may have felt toward the king. George III's refusal to review Lee's request for promotion did little to assauge his ire. During the years 1767-68, Lee's letters supporting the marquis of Rockingham and John Wilkes inevitably meant that his political views would continue to obstruct his ambitions in England.

As he had so frequently done in the past, Lee refused to remain idle. He returned to the Continent in 1768, hoping to secure a command in the Russian army, which was then engaged in a war with the Ottoman Empire. He was appointed a major general in the Polish army by Stanislas, who was beleaguered by enemies within the Polish confederation. Lee used his new honorary title when he reached the Russian army at Chotin in Bessarabia. He served as an unofficial observer at this bloody but inconsequential battle and failed to secure the appointment he desired. He was incapacitated by illness for several months; his health returned slowly as he traveled from Vienna to Florence. After visiting Sicily he returned to London in June 1771.

Lee's biographer, John Richard Alden, attributes the increasing venom in his letters to this lingering illness, as well as chronic bouts with gout and rheumatism.[12] There is no doubt that Lee continued to support American resistance while in eastern Europe and on his return. He castigated the policies of Lord North as tyrannical and corrupt. In contrast, he observed that "America has . . . a chance of emerging from ministerial oppression; on this I fix my hopes."[13] On his return to Great Britain he quickly took up his pen to publish an essay praising the Holy Roman Emperor Joseph II, for attempting to serve the interests of his people. He also wrote an essay about the British monarch that bordered on sedition. Clearly Lee was courting political martyrdom in enunciating his Whig ideas, even though his criticisms only mirrored those of other Britons of similar ideological bent.

For the next two years, while recuperating, Lee visited friends and traveled to France. Even he admitted, "My chief amusement is disgorging part of my spleen on paper."[14] His last letters from Europe reveal a desire to escape either to the democratic cantons of Switzerland or to America, where there was "some climate and soil more friendly to the spirit of liberty."[15]

Lee's move to America was motivated by more than a desire for political asylum or military advancement. He had received a promotion to lieutenant colonel in 1772 and had invested substantially in Florida and Prince Edward Island. He left England in August 1773 for a variety of reasons: resentment, love of military adventure, Whig politics and, possibly, finances. Charles Lee was a perfect candidate for a budding American revolutionary. Lee now preferred the uncertain virtues of America to the well-known vices of Hanoverian England.

Arriving in New York City on October 8, 1773, Lee behaved much more like an English gentleman on tour than a refugee seeking political asylum. Before setting out to visit the southern colonies he spent several weeks in the city. He traveled through Philadelphia to the Eastern Shore of Virginia and eventually reached Williamsburg in the spring of 1774. Lee was vacationing during what proved to be the last period of calm in the thirteen colonies for a decade. During his visit to the planter capital, news of the passage of the Boston Port Bill was received. By that time Lee had already become acquainted with several of the colony's leading spokesmen in opposition to Great Britain—Thomas Jefferson, George Mason, and Richard Henry Lee (no relation). Charles Lee is credited with aiding colonial leaders to promote a day of fast in support of the people of Boston. The Virginia House of Burgesses subsequently passed a resolution calling for a day of fast. Writing to Horatio Gates, an old correspondent and future comrade in arms, Lee asked, "What think you of our blessed Ministry—do they not improve in absurdity and wickedness? . . . for my own part I am determin'd (at least I think I am) not to be slack in whatever mode my service is required."[16]

Lee resumed his perambulations and, like a moth drawn toward the flame of resistance and rebellion, returned to Philadelphia. Under the pseudonym of "Anglus Americanus" he wrote an address to the citizens of Philadelphia that urged concerted colonial action, envisioning America's protest as the start of a counterattack on British despotism. In July 1774 he composed a similar panegyric for the consumption of New York readers.[17] There is little doubt that the rising prerevolutionary movement ideally suited a man of Lee's candor and vitriolic disdain for the ministry and king of Great Britain. In this instance his harsh words added to his reputation instead of acting as a further impediment. As colonists began to call for a continental congress, his old acquaintances in the British civil and military establishment were concerned and curious about his sympathy with American grievances.

Lee completed what was, for its time, the grand tour of America by traveling to the center of revolutionary sentiment, New England. Reaching Boston in August 1774, he became the political friend of Joseph Warren, Samuel Adams and John Hancock. In a letter to General Thomas Gage, the military commander of the city, retired Lieutenant Colonel Charles Lee showed that he had begun to share the American viewpoint that liberty had been driven from Great Britain "by a damn'd conspiracy of Kings and Ministers . . . here is her last asylum."[18] In letters to his British friends Lee wrote of the unity of the American colonists. In a letter to Hugh, Earl Percy, he defended his behavior as arising "not from any pique and disappointment (which I conclude will be insinuated) but from principle."[19] He left Boston for Philadelphia on August 17.

Many of the delegates attending the First Continental Congress may have envied Lee's sudden prominence. He spent much of September and October socializing in Philadelphia. There he met George Washington, whom he might first have met during the French and Indian War. If Lee entertained military ambitions, he certainly pursued them with his usual avidity. He drafted a proposal for an American army, read by such influential politicians as John Adams and Thomas Jefferson.[20]

While he remained in Philadelphia, Lee once again propagandized for the American cause. He composed a stinging rebuttal to the Friendly Address to All Reasonable Americans, written by the Reverend Dr. Myles Cooper, the president of King's College. Cooper's piece blamed the American disturbance on a few factious leaders who misguided the colonists, and he warned his readers of the superior force of the British army. Lee composed his Strictures on . . . A Friendly Address to assure the anxious colonists of the justice of their cause and of the strength they possessed to resist Great Britain. He reassured the Americans of their capacity to fight what he called a civil war and dismissed the possibility that numerous German mercenaries would come to America to crush a rebellion. He portrayed the British army as "composed of the most debauched Weavers' 'prentices, the scum of the Irish Roman Catholics, who desert upon every occasion, and a few Scotch, who are not strong enough to carry packs."[21] He lauded the performance of the American militia in the French and Indian War and pressed for a general plan for military training. He assured the colonists that their field officers were as capable as British officers, concluding that "being prepared for a civil war is the surest means of preventing it."[22] This piece was reprinted and read widely. Although Alden may overestimate Lee's importance in these years, he is certainly astute in observing that "it is not to be doubted that his writings, his conversation, and his very presence in America contributed to the rising tide of anti-British sentiment."[23]

The next few months were portentous ones for the retired Lieutenant Colonel Charles Lee and for America. In the fall of 1774 Lee traveled south once again and, on two different occasions, visited George Washington at Mount Vernon. His visit to Washington's estate in April 1775 may have included a discussion of formal military preparations. The visit coincided with the battles of Lexington and Concord. The formation of an American army was the major item on the agenda of the Second Continental Congress in May 1775. That month Lee returned to Philadelphia, where he was available for any post to be offered. Earlier he had disclaimed any pretense of becoming the commander in chief, but he began to publicize his undeniable military experience. On June 17, 1775, Congress selected George Washington to be commander in chief. In an unusual display of nonsectional voting, the

New England delegates swung the voting to a Virginian. After much private debate, Lee, with Washington's support, was appointed major general and third in command after Artemas Ward. He accepted the post only after he had conferred with a committee to compensate him for the financial losses he had suffered in relinquishing his British commission.

In Lee's letter, dated June 22, 1775, resigning his lieutenant colonel's commission, he remarked that "as a citizen, Englishman, and soldier of a free state," he would fight for the rights and liberties of his adopted land.[24] On June 23, when he left Philadelphia with his commander to assume the leadership of the Continental army, Lee had seemingly completed his commitment to American resistance. The next two years would determine whether this commitment was to American independence or to peaceful reconciliation with Great Britain. In other words, was Charles Lee an expatriate eighteenth-century English Commonwealthman or an American fighting for his country?

The high command of the American army arrived in Massachusetts in July 1775. The Provincial Congress of Massachusetts welcomed Charles Lee on July 1. In his reply he assured the delegates that they could depend on his "zeal and integrity."[25] Lee quickly addressed himself to supervising the fortifications and readiness of the troops at Prospect Hill. The American army, from its positions overlooking the city of Boston, began an artillery bombardment that dislodged the British nearly a year later. Letters of his contemporaries cite the value to the untested army of Lee's military experience. For once, he rarely quarreled with other officers. He felt it was his "duty as a citizen and asserter of liberty, to waive every consideration."[26]

However, Lee's inability to avoid expounding his Whig principles to his former comrades in the British army caused several incidents, one of which was fatal to his career as a major general. In several letters, Lee engaged in an Anglo-American dialogue with his former commander, General John Burgoyne (who shared some of Lee's political opinions). Although Burgoyne professed to be aware of the political theory of John Locke, he maintained that the Americans masked their desire for independence in the guise of constitutional problems. He offered to meet Lee privately to convey some letters and discuss the imperial crisis further. For once Lee wisely consulted the Provincial Congress of Massachusetts about the possible meeting. After that body counseled him to reject the overture, Lee wrote Burgoyne "that the interview might create those jealousies and suspicions so natural to a people struggling in the dearest of all causes, that of their liberty, property, wives, children, and their future generation."[27]

Lee's letter from camp to Richard Henry Lee on December 12, 1775, contained a personal statement on the future course of politics and military action. He advised seizing and disarming royal governors such as Lord Dunmore of Virginia and William Tryon of New York, fully comprehending that their presence was a Loyalist rallying point. He recommended confiscation of Loyalists' property and advocated the strong fortification of New York City and Charleston. (Time proved Lee correct. When the British attacked both cities in 1776, inadequate fortifications caused major defensive problems.) American civil and military leaders were learning to listen to Lee's views despite their presentation in letters full, as he himself admitted, of "self-conceit and egotism."[28]

Lee's proposal to fortify New York and suppress the Loyalists there brought about the first strain in his relationship with George Washington. On January 5, 1776, Lee wrote Washington that he had "scarcely been able to sleep from apprehensions" of the enemy capturing the city. The New York Committee of Public Safety's dilatory behavior and Governor William Tryon's presence aboard a ship in New York harbor complicated the problem. Lee believed that Congress was reluctant to act in its turn for fear of infringing on the authority of a colony. Characteristically, Lee advised Washington to exercise his mandate to take decisive action: "You have it in your power, at present, to prevent this dreadful event. If I do not mistake, the Congress have given you authority to take any step."[29] On January 8, Washington responded by informing

Lee of a probable movement of the British fleet at Boston on a "southern expedition"—a campaign aimed at New York. He ignored Lee's impertinence and suggested that Lee take volunteers from Connecticut and New Jersey to prepare for the defense of the city—precisely the plan Lee had proposed.[30] The exchange was clearly an example of the brash Lee being shrewdly manipulated by his commander.

Lee thrived in situations where he operated with little interference from his superiors. Aware of Lee's reputation for decisive action, the New York Committee of Public Safety wrote to him on January 21, defending their preparations and asking him not to come with his volunteers until he explained his course of action. Lee responded with harsh rhetoric. He told the committee that he had no desire to engage the British ships that entered the harbor on January 20. He declared, however, "if they make a pretext of my presence to fire on the Town the first house set in flames by their Guns shall be the funeral pile of some of their best friends."[31] Lee proposed to the Continental Congress a way to end the problem of Loyalism. He urged confiscation of Loyalist arms and a forced oath of allegiance secured by half their property.

In New York Lee worked quite well with a committee of the Continental Congress to prepare the city for an imminent British attack. Arriving on February 4, he wisely fortified the avenues of possible retreat to Kingsbridge and the guard at the harbor and the East River. Lee's plans for the defense of narrow Manhattan Island avoided concentrating large bodies of troops for fear of being encircled and cut off from the mainland. He gathered a force of twenty-five hundred men for this task. Although Lee admitted Washington had not given him the power to do so, he "most impudently" appointed Isaac Sears as adjutant general with the rank of lieutenant colonel for an expedition to administer oaths to the Tories of Long Island. Lee stressed that the small British force under General Sir Henry Clinton that sailed into the harbor on February 4 was only a prelude to a massive attack.

On February 17, 1776, the Continental Congress appointed Lee to command the American forces in Canada. He received the appointment because of his energy and reputation in Congress, achieved through the influence of such friends as Robert Morris and Edward Rutledge. The Canadian expedition of 1775 led by General Richard Montgomery and Colonel Benedict Arnold had stalled before Quebec after a bloody and unsuccessful attack on the city on December 31, 1775. John Adams wrote to Lee on February 19, "We want you at N. York—We want you at Cambridge—We want you in Virginia—But Canada seems of more Importance than any of those places, and therefore you are sent there."[32] However, on March 1, 1776, after a successful protest by southern delegates, the Continental Congress changed its mind and appointed him commander of the newly created Southern Department. In a letter to George Washington on March 3, Lee remarked, "As I am the only General Officer on the Continental who can speak and think in French, I confess it would have been more prudent to have sent me to Canada, but I shall obey with alacrity, and hope with success."[33] Lee reached Philadelphia on March 11 to consult the Continental Congress and provided them a report on the implementation of his plans for the defense of New York City. Again he stressed that the presence of an active group of Tories on Long Island and Staten Island would be fatal to the defense of the region. He suggested that the children of the disaffected be held as hostages for their good behavior.

By March 20, Lee reached Baltimore on his way to assume what was to be an almost independent command, for he was subordinate only to the Continental Congress. His actions in the South, therefore, indicate his personal military skills and his abilities under fire. Lee spent April and early May in Williamsburg. He acted with military shrewdness and his usual impetuosity. He quickly assessed his defenses and the available supply of provisions and munitions. He perceived that the number of accessible rivers unprotected by American ships made defense of Virginia and the lower South a problem. He began the tedious process of requesting supplies and men from the Virginia Council of Safety. Lee's suspicion that Lord Dunmore's occupation of Norfolk would encourage the Tories prompted his request that the Council of Safety send the local inhabitants inland. The council denied his request to hold the women and children hostage. If Lee exceeded his authority ordering the Baltimore Committee of Safety to seize Robert Eden, the governor of Maryland, there was nothing wrong with his military acumen. His plans for the defense of Virginia and North Carolina helped them prepare for an imminent British attack. On May 8 he received word that a large British fleet had been sighted off the North Carolina coast, and he moved south. By May 25 he learned that Charleston was the probable British destination. This relieved his anxiety about the amount of territory he had to defend. As he had remarked to a North Carolina general, "it is my duty to superintend the Security and Safety of four wide extended Provinces, the enemy being furnished with canvass wings can fly with expedition from one quarter to ano[the]r."[34]

The British arrived at Charleston on June 4. The firepower of the warships in Sir Peter Parker's fleet was enormous. It far surpassed that of the artillery in the fortifications on Sullivan's Island, which protected the entrance to Charleston harbor. The warships escorted approximately thirty transports carrying Clinton's twenty-five hundred troops. Lee commanded a force of state troops, militia and about two thousand Continental soldiers from North Carolina and Virginia. However, as in New York in February, the town's defenses were inadequate and incomplete. Lee's primary concerns were to complete the fortifications and impede the British at every point. In his June 6 and 8 letters to Colonel William Moultrie, commanding the main American position on Sullivan's Island, Lee ordered riflemen sent to the adjacent Long Island and adequate preparations for their withdrawal by boat.[35] While the British fleet prepared for battle, Lee was busy refining his defensive strategy. At Haddrell's Point (about halfway between Sullivan's Island and Charleston, on the north shore of the harbor) he arranged for fortifications from which to harass the British if they succeeded in passing the guns of Sullivan's Island and to protect an American retreat. In this emergency, his terse orders to his officers demanded instant obedience. In a letter to Colonel Christopher

Gadsden, Lee advised that should a British naval force pass his post, "not a single Gun will be fired at too great a distance—not a single Gun, but when you have the greatest probability of its being fired with effect."[36] On June 21, Lee wrote to Colonel William Thompson, chiding him for permitting his men communication with the enemy.[37]

Lee was convinced that overreliance on Fort Sullivan would commit too much artillery, which would be useless once the British had passed the fort. Moreover, he was not certain the fort could be defended. He met with John Rutledge, the president of South Carolina, to explain his misgivings. Lee accepted Rutledge's decision that the fort could be defended, and he moved quickly to help buttress it for the imminent attack.

On the morning of June 28, the British fleet attempted to force Charleston harbor and subjected the fort on Sullivan's Island to a savage bombardment. Lee remarked that it was "one of the most furious cannonades I ever heard or saw."[38] However, Fort Sullivan was constructed largely of palmetto logs, whose peculiar properties countered the deadly bombardment. The soft and spongy wood absorbed the cannon balls and rendered them harmless. The tide of battle turned when three British ships ran aground and the fort's cannon damaged several others. By nine in the evening the British attack ended. Lee congratulated Moultrie for his successful defense of the harbor. In a series of letters to Horatio Gates and Benjamin Rush, Lee expressed his amazement at the skills of the untrained men. In a July 1 letter to George Washington, he confessed, "The cool courage they displayed astonished and enraptured me."[39] Lee ordered his men to remain alert, fearing the June 28 assault was but the first of several. However, damage to the fleet and the British decision to recall it to attack New York temporarily freed the South from the threat of British invasion.

The American victory at Charleston had three ingredients: British errors and misfortunes, American gallantry and the generalship of Charles Lee. Many military historians have analyzed his decisions at Charleston. Lee, for once, controlled his temper and devoted all his energies to preparations for a major conflict. His presence and stature were, in part, responsible for the discipline and efficiency of his troops under fire. As William Moultrie later wrote, Lee's cooperation with the South Carolina troops under Moultrie and with John Rutledge enabled him to keep control of the complex military situation. His initial belief that Fort Sullivan was indefensible arose from the usual difficulties faced by a Continental commander: an enemy superior in numbers, training and materiel.

While Lee remained in Charleston, the main American army under George Washington was stationed in New York City. After urgent appeals for troops, Washington had scraped together an army of twenty thousand. On July 3, a large British fleet began to land thousands of troops on Staten Island in preparation for a major conflict. Congress and the army turned to Lee for leadership. Colonel John Dickinson wrote to Lee from Elizabethtown: "I wish you were here to direct our operations in this affair—As far as I can judge, a good deal of Generalship will be necessary for giving success to the measure."[40] With Clinton's return to New York in late July the Americans expected an imminent attack. John Hancock, president of Congress, wrote to Lee on August 18, recalling him to Philadelphia for further orders. Lee arrived in Philadelphia by October 7.

By the time Lee reached the North the American position around New York City had deteriorated. The battle of Long Island on August 27-28, 1776, brought a major defeat and the near loss of an American force at Brooklyn Heights. The British attack on Manhattan that began on September 15 left the American army commanding only the upper end of the island. Such a train of events and losses gave Lee the stature of a victorious general who could be looked to to turn the tide. Though ordered to Harlem Heights on October 7 to rejoin Washington, he was allowed to inspect the defenses in New Jersey and report his findings. Lee found the concentration of the American army in New York State deplorable. On October 12 he wrote to Congress from Perth Amboy that he suspected a British thrust toward Philadelphia to exploit this situation. As always, Lee was candid. On his arrival at Fort Constitution (Fort Lee) he wrote to

Horatio Gates, "inter nos the Congress seem to stumble at every step . . . I have been very free in delivering my opinion to 'em—in my opinion General Washington is much to blame in not menacing 'em with resignation."[41] Because letters were easily intercepted, this comment could have been politically embarrassing and explosive. Once again, Lee failed to consider this possibility. Lee's fear of a possible British flanking move at Throg's Neck may have contributed to Washington's decision to withdraw from Manhattan Island.[42]

Lee was stationed at White Plains after the inconclusive battle there on October 28. In a letter to Colonel Joseph Reed on the day Fort Washington fell (November 16), he wrote that the decision to pen up so many fine troops for capture was a grave mistake.[43] On November 20 the British crossed the Hudson River into New Jersey and attacked Fort Lee, the American redoubt on the Palisades. Lee had to guard against a British advance northward while Washington was to check the enemy on the western side of the Hudson. On November 21, the day after Fort Lee fell, Washington ordered him to cross the Hudson in an attempt to concentrate American forces in New Jersey.

During this crisis, Lee reverted to making his own discretionary judgments. He wrote to Reed that he was unable to cross the river easily at Dobbs Ferry and would only detach two thousand troops from General William Heath, for "withdrawing our Troops from hence, would be attended with some very serious consequences."[44] Heath, on the other hand, adhered strictly to the intent of Washington's orders and counseled Lee to do the same. Lee derided Heath for his fidelity to orders from his commanding officers, concluding, "the Commander in Chief is now separated from us, that I of course command on this side the Water, that for the future I must and will be obey'd."[45] While the wrangling over the intent of orders continued, Washington's army retreated through New Jersey. Lee defended his inaction, but Washington had already reached Trenton before Lee had finally crossed the Hudson on November 30. By December 8 Lee had reached Morristown with twenty-seven hundred men. Washington wrote on December 10 that his army was undermanned and urgently requested Lee to join him. Writing to Horatio Gates from Basking Ridge on December 12-13, Lee unleashed his frustration over his situation: "entre nous, a certain great man is most damnably deficient,—He has thrown me into a situation where I have my choice of difficulties . . . . We are lost—our Counsels have been weak to the last degree."[46] There was little for Lee to do at this moment, for within hours he had become the prisoner of a party of British dragoons led by Lieutenant Colonel William Harcourt.

Lee blamed his capture on "the fortune of war, the activity of Colonel Harcourt, and the rascality of my own troops."[47] However, it was Lee who decided to spend the night at Basking Ridge, accompanied only by a small escort. Lee was plainly negligent, because Morris County was a no-man's land where only the constant protection of one's troops was sufficient for safety.

Lee's eighteen months of captivity in New York City was a sorry period in his career. On December 20, 1776, the Continental Congress sent money for his use and inquired about his welfare. On January 6, Congress resolved to protest Lee's reported confinement. Congress offered to exchange Lee for five Hessian officers captured at Trenton and a British lieutenant colonel. From January to June 1777, Lee occupied comfortable quarters and was well treated. In June he was placed aboard a British warship, where he remained until December 27, when he was paroled but confined to the city. The British, after much discussion, considered him a retired British officer and an American prisoner of war, not a British traitor. Lee was sent to Philadelphia, where he arrived on March 25, 1778. On April 5, he signed a parole and departed for American lines.

During Lee's confinement he made ineffectual efforts to end the war. On February 10, 1777, he wrote to John Hancock that he wished several representatives from Congress would come to New York to discuss subjects "what so deeply interest myself & in my opinion the Community."[48] Most members of Congress wisely refused to respond positively since Lee's proposal may have been a British trap. On March 29, 1777, the Continental Congress resolved not to send a committee to negotiate with Sir William Howe, British commander in chief. In March Lee submitted a plan to British authorities. It included statements that America could not win the war and that "she must in the end, after great desolation havock and slaughter, be reduc'd to submit to terms much harder than might probably be granted at present."[49] To shorten the war, he then proposed a series of British attacks on several colonies. Although his biographer suggests that the plan may have been a ruse to confuse British strategies, had the document fallen into American hands, Lee would have been branded a traitor. In 1778 he appealed for the end of hostilities because both sides would suffer from a continuation of the war.

With his final exchange on April 21 for British Major General Richard Prescott, Lee resumed an active role in the American army. He arrived at Valley Forge on May 21 and resumed his place as second in command. On May 22, 1778, he and several other ranking officers counseled Washington that the weakness of the Continental army made an offensive against the British impossible. On June 17, after the British evacuation of Philadelphia became a certainty, Washington called a council of war. Lee and the majority advised Washington to avoid a major confrontation in New Jersey. A second conference on June 24 reached the same conclusion. With the appointment of the marquis de Lafayette as the commander of all forward elements following the British across the state, Lee protested this slight to his rank and seniority. Washington tactfully ended the dispute quickly, and Lee was in command on the morning of June 28 near Monmouth Court House.

What do the life and career of Charles Lee before the battle of Monmouth tell us of the events of June 28? Even a man of so many moods and temper operated within fixed patterns. He was a proud, vain, egotistical man who rarely refrained from expressing his anger and frustration over the lack of consideration given his political viewpoints and military strategy. He considered himself an able, wise and courageous officer and brooked little opposition when in command. He found it difficult to accept subordinate positions and was more effective as an independent commander. Militarily he was conservative. Though his preference for defense would have sustained the American army in the field, it would have crippled the morale of the troops and the citizenry. Washington, aware of the importance of morale, disregarded his officers' advice and decided to attack at Monmouth. Lee found the tide of protest and resistance in America compatible with his Whig views of the despotism of king and Parliament. However, he continued to believe that the crisis could be reconciled—even after independence and bloodshed. He had a poor opinion of both his army and its commander in chief, which he expressed with little tact and less discretion. His behavior at Monmouth conformed to the pattern of his long career as British officer, Whig politician and American general.

NOTES

1. Most of Charles Lee's surviving papers are printed in The Lee Papers, Collections of the New-York Historical Society . . . , 4 vols. (New York, 1872-75). They are cited hereafter as LP. The original documents were either lost or destroyed after publication. Other Lee papers are in The Papers of The Continental Congress at the National Archives, Washington, D.C., and The Papers of George Washington at the Library of Congress, Washington, D.C.
2. The most balanced appraisal of Lee's life is John Richard Alden, General Charles Lee: Traitor or Patriot? (Baton Rouge: Louisiana State University Press, 1951).
3. Alden, Lee, pp. 5-6, ascribes the coolness between Lee and his mother to the "eccentricity" emanating from the mother's family. He cites heredity as the basis for Lee's lifelong "moodiness and choleric temper."
4. Charles Lee to Sidney Lee, June 18, 1756, LP, 1:2-6.
5. Lee to Sidney Lee, September 16, 1758, ibid., 1:7.
6. Ibid.
7. Lee to Sidney Lee, February 6, 1767, ibid., 1:51-52.
8. Alden, Lee, pp. 23-24.
9. Lee to Sir Charles Burnbury, December 7, 1764, LP, 1:36.
10. Lee to the earl of Charlemont, June 1, 1765, ibid., 1:40.
11. Lee to Sidney Lee, March 1, 1766, ibid., 1:43.
12. Alden, Lee, p. 38.
13. Lee to Sir Charles Davers, December 24, 1769, LP, 1:91.
14. Lee to Sidney Lee, March 28, 1772, ibid., 1:111.
15. Lee to Davers, March 26, 1772, ibid., 1:108.
16. Lee to Horatio Gates, May 6, 1774, ibid., 1:122.
17. Alden, Lee, pp. 53-54.
18. Lee to Thomas Gage, 1774, LP, 1:134.
19. Lee to Earl Percy, 1775, ibid., 1:171.
20. Alden, Lee, p. 61.
21. "Strictures on a Pamphlet entitled 'A Friendly Address to All Reasonable Americans, on the Subject of our Political Confusions,' " LP, 1:161.
22. Ibid., 1:165.
23. Alden, Lee, p. 65.
24. Lee to Lord Barrington, June 22, 1775, LP, 1:186.
25. Lee to the Provincial Congress of Massachusetts, July 1, 1775, ibid., 1:187.
26. Lee to John Thomas, July 23, 1775, ibid., 1:198.
27. Lee to John Burgoyne, July 11, 1775, ibid., 1:194.
28. Lee to Richard Henry Lee, December 12, 1775, ibid., 1:229.
29. Lee to George Washington, January 5, 1776, ibid., 1:234.
30. Washington to Lee, January 8, 1776, ibid., 1:236-37.
31. Lee to Peter V.B. Livingston, January 23, 1776, ibid., 1:257.
32. John Adams to Lee, February 19, 1776, ibid., 1:312.
33. Lee to Washington, March 3, 1776, ibid., 1:343.
34. Lee to James Moore, May 20, 1776, ibid., 2:31.
35. Lee to William Moultrie, June 6, 8, 1776, ibid., 2:55-56.
36. Lee to Christopher Gadsden, June 19, 1776, ibid., 2:75.
37. Lee to William Thompson, June 21, 1776, ibid., 2:76-77.
38. Lee to the president of the Convention of Virginia, June 29, 1776, ibid., 2:93.
39. Lee to Washington, July 1, 1776, ibid., 2:101.
40. John Dickinson to Lee, July 25, 1776, ibid., 2:168.
41. Lee to Gates, October 14, 1776, ibid., 2:261-62.
42. Alden, Lee, p. 144.
43. Lee to Joseph Reed, November 16, 1776, LP, 2:283-84.
44. Lee to Reed, November 21, 1776, ibid., 2:301.
45. Lee to William Heath, November 26, 1776, ibid., 2:314.
46. Lee to Gates, December 12-13, 1776, ibid., 2:348.
47. Lee to Primrose Kennedy, December 1776, ibid., 2:356.
48. Lee to John Hancock, February 10, 1777, ibid., 2:358.
49. "Scheme for Putting an End to the War, Submitted to the Royal Commissioners, 29th March, 1777," ibid., 2:361.

CHARLES LEE'S ACTIONS
AT THE BATTLE OF MONMOUTH:
A PANEL OF HISTORIANS

Samuel S. Smith, Chairman

Charles Lee at the
Battle of Monmouth:
An Introduction to the Question

Samuel S. Smith

Our panel discussion today is titled "Charles Lee's Actions at the Battle of Monmouth." As is well known, General Lee was court-martialed for his actions that day, June 28, 1778.

The charges against Lee were

> First: For disobedience of orders, in not attacking the enemy on the 28th of June, agreeable with repeated instructions.
> Secondly: For misbehavior before the enemy on the same day, by making an <u>unnecessary, disorderly and shameful retreat.</u>
> Thirdly: For disrespect to the Commander in Chief, in two letters dated the 1st July and 28th of June.[1]

Lee was found guilty as charged on the first and third counts. But in finding Lee guilty of the second charge, the court altered its wording to read "misbehavior before the enemy on the 28th of June, by making an unnecessary, and in some few instances, a disorderly retreat . . . "[2]

I presume the first two charges will be discussed by members of the panel and by the audience, at the proper time. The first charge is quite straightforward. The third charge involves letters written after the battle and does not appear to concern us today. The second charge seems to call for a review of what happened that day while Lee was in command of forward troops.

The American army had spent the winter of 1777-78 at Valley Forge, while the British occupied Philadelphia, the capital of the United States, some forty-five miles from Valley Forge. The winter had brought good news for the American cause: the French government would enter the war against the British.

When the British learned of the intended French intervention, they decided to evacuate Philadelphia and concentrate their forces at New York, which they also held. General Washington was soon informed through his spy system that the British intended to make this move. But it took several weeks of anxious waiting before he learned when the move would begin and if the enemy would travel by land or by sea.

On June 18 the British commander in chief, Lieutenant General Sir Henry Clinton, crossed the Delaware River from Philadelphia with twelve thousand men, and began his long march across New Jersey toward New York. Within a matter of hours Washington, with his army of about the same strength, was on the march to intercept them. By June 27 the British were at Freehold and the Americans were at Englishtown, only five miles away.

At 6:00 a.m. on June 28, as ordered, General Lee, with roughly four thousand men—nearly one-third of the American army—marched from Englishtown toward Freehold to engage the enemy. Lee and his force reached the town around noon and saw the last of the British leaving Freehold on the road to Middletown and Sandy Hook. Lee judged this rear guard to number perhaps five hundred men and ordered Brigadier General Anthony Wayne to attack it with his force of about six hundred.

As Wayne marched to the attack, Lee spotted another two thousand British and promptly sent orders to Wayne to withdraw to Freehold, intending to lure both bodies of the enemy into a trap. The trap would be sprung after Lee made a circling movement to attack the British from the rear.

When Lee arrived at a position just south of Lake Topanemus, he found that Wayne had not withdrawn to Freehold but had continued his pursuit of the rear guard. Wayne's motion brought the two American forces together again.

Lee then formed a line and went out to reconnoiter. He saw another body of the enemy, which he judged to be about five thousand strong, forming on Briar Hill, directly in front of Lee's line. Soon this force began to move toward the Americans and Lee ordered his cannon into action.

While the cannonade continued, two artillery pieces in Wayne's command ran out of ammunition and their commander withdrew from the line. This movement triggered the withdrawal of several infantry regiments on the other end of the American line, and the entire formation began to crumble. With his line falling apart and the enemy moving toward Freehold, Lee fell back on the town in an effort to stop them.

In the confusion some elements of the American force became separated. While some American units took a position on Monument Hill, Lee withdrew to Carr's House where he believed his whole force could fight effectively. But in the withdrawal about fourteen hundred men of the Monument Hill force took a route that prevented them from joining Lee.

With his strength now reduced to around twenty-six hundred men, against an advancing British force of three times that number, Lee ordered a further withdrawal. As his force crossed the West Morass Causeway, Lee and Washington met.

There was a sharp exchange of words between the two men. Washington ordered Lee to recross the causeway and hold the enemy until Washington could form a line of defense. In the ensuing action Lee delayed the British long enough for Washington to send troops and artillery to Combs Hill and to another hill position overlooking the causeway. When the British again drove Lee back across the causeway, the American artillery was able to counter their attack.

After a two-hour cannonade and two British attempts to take the causeway, the enemy fell back to Carr's House. Washington pursued with a large force but darkness brought the fighting to a halt. During the night the enemy slipped away toward Sandy Hook and safety.

In conclusion I wish to pose two questions. Both questions are based on Lee's court-martial verdict. They are, first, was Lee guilty of "disobeying orders" at Monmouth and were such orders "repeatedly given" to him? Second, did Lee make an "unnecessary and in some few instances disorderly retreat?"

NOTES

1. Proceedings of A General Court-Martial . . . for the Trial of Major-General Lee, July 4th, 1778 (New York, 1864), p. 4.
2. Ibid., p. 238.

Washington's Strategic Intentions for the Battle of Monmouth

Russell F. Weigley

One means of shedding light on the vexing questions raised by George Washington's and Charles Lee's conduct of the battle of Monmouth might be to view the battle in terms of its place in the American strategy for winning the revolutionary war. In Carl von Clausewitz's definition, strategy teaches "the use of engagements for the object of the war," as distinguished from tactics, which "teaches the use of armed forces in the engagement."[1] The military strategist attempts to fit a single engagement or battle such as Monmouth, into a larger scheme of developments that will add up to winning the war in which he is involved. From the strategic perspective, the question Washington's conduct of the battle of Monmouth raises is, how did Washington intend this engagement to contribute to achieving the object of the war?

Discussing Monmouth from a strategic perspective is awkward because Washington may never have heard the word strategy. The term entered military discourse during his lifetime. To the limited extent of its use before the nineteenth century, it retained much of the sense of stratagem, a ruse, rather than the larger definitions given it by Clausewitz and other interpreters of Napoleonic warfare. Nevertheless, Washington surely went into his battles with some notion of how he hoped each might contribute to the desired outcome of the war. Recent-ly, we have had a book-length study of Washington as strategist: Colonel Dave Richard Palmer's The Way of the Fox[2]. The fox of the title, of course, is Washington. Palmer believes Washington's revolutionary war strategy falls into four phases; Monmouth fits into the third, the climactic and especially aggressive phase. In the first phase, from April 1775 to July 1776, revolutionary strategy was nearly as aggressive. It was also at its most successful. The British were ejected from every mainland American province south of Canada and north of Florida. In the second phase, from July 1776 to December 1777, a formidable British army attempting to reconquer the lost provinces put the revolutionaries on the defensive. It occupied much of New York and New Jersey along with Newport and Philadelphia, and would have achieved more had it not been for Washington's skilled generalship. In Palmer's third phase, from January 1778 to December 1781, France's intervention threw the British on the defensive and permitted Washington to return to the offensive. This phase reached its climax at the battle of Yorktown, which assured the independence of the United States. In the final phase, January 1782 to December 1783, the Americans attempted to maintain both their tenuous grip on the Northwest and their bargaining position until the final peace.

Palmer implies that Monmouth was an

effort by Washington to begin the destruction of the British army. He says that the nature of the third phase of the war was such that

> military victory became possible. The invaders could be decisively beaten, could be driven off American soil. Moreover, risks could be more freely taken, for the loss now of a major portion of the Continental army would not necessarily be fatal; the Revolution had taken too firm a hold in the country to be rooted out by an England also at war with France. Seizing the initiative was Washington's new imperative, defeating the British army his overriding goal.[3]

In this context, Palmer writes more specifically of Monmouth: "The general [Washington] convened a council of war on 24 June. Should the Continentals hazard a general action? If so, should it be a major assault, a partial one, or should they maneuver in such a way as to make the British attack?" Palmer goes on to describe how Major General Charles Lee's desire to "avoid all action and wait for the French to enter the war" led the council to vote narrowly against attack. Palmer resumes:

> That night, Wayne, Lafayette, and Greene each wrote to Washington urging him to overrule the council and attack anyway. Realizing that a chance was slipping through his fingers—one that might never again be repeated—the general decided to take the bolder course. He gave Lafayette command of the advance detachment and set his entire army in motion on the road to Monmouth Court House.[4]

Though Palmer does not explicitly say so, he clearly implies that in overruling the council, Washington had decided not only on an attack but on a "general action," believing that "the invaders could be decisively beaten, could be driven off American soil." In this view, Washington went into battle at Monmouth willing to take on the whole British army in a "general action" of both armies.

Palmer may be right, both about Washington's strategy through the later years of the war and about his intentions at Monmouth in particular. But my own reading of Washington's strategy differs from Palmer's and leads to a different conception of what Washington probably intended at Monmouth. Agreed, Washington was aggressive enough in the first months of the war when, for example, he supported the effort to conquer Canada. During Palmer's second phase Washington was still willing to engage the main weight of the British army in open combat—until the battles around New York in 1776 showed him the true dimensions of the qualitative superiority of the British army. Thereafter, he risked his army in open battle against the British main force only in the most unusual circumstances. I do not believe Washington's strategy was ever as aggressive as Palmer posits for the period January 1778–December 1781.

Despite the French alliance, Washington never in that period acted on the belief that the "invaders could be decisively beaten, could be driven off American soil," except in the Yorktown campaign, when a French fleet and army were operating in immediate and direct cooperation with him. Unless the French were an immediate physical presence, Washington learned early in the alliance what he wisely suspected from the beginning; since he could not count on their cooperation with the Continental army he must still rely on American resources. If he still had to rely primarily on American resources, it was not true that "risks could be more freely taken, for the loss now of a major portion of the Continental Army would not necessarily be fatal." Rather, such a loss would still be fatal. The Revolution had not taken the firm hold Palmer supposes. The history of the Revolution from 1778 to 1781 is one of a gradually faltering cause beset by ruinous financial inflation, inability to supply or recruit an adequate army, and worst, the accumulating loss of confidence in the revolutionary cause among the American people. Increasingly, the British command perceived the Americans' cause as lost. Washington's letters make it clear that he shared this view. And it may well have been that without the extraordinary good fortune of Yorktown, the Revolution might well have faded away.

Washington's strategy from 1778 through the end of the war was no different from that of 1776. In September 1776, aware of the limitations of his army, he clearly defined his strategy.

> In deliberating on this Question [of the proper revolutionary strategy], it was impossible to forget, that History, our own

experience, the advice of our ablest Friends in Europe, the fears of the Enemy, and even the Declarations of Congress demonstrate, that on our Side the War should be defensive. It has even been called a War of Posts. That we should on all Occasions avoid a general Action, or put anything to the Risque, unless compelled by a necessity, into which we ought never to be drawn.[5]

As Washington perceived it, the Continental army was essential to the life of the Revolution. Therefore the army must be kept alive and must not be risked unduly. It must fight a defensive war, without the risk of major battles. The hope of eventual victory must lie in the gradual erosion of support for the war in the British Parliament and cabinet so that in the end there could be a negotiated peace recognizing American independence.

The Continental army never grew strong enough for Washington to expect more from it than he did when he defined his defensive strategy in 1776. As late as the summer of 1780, he described his strategic plans as still bound to a dreary cycle:

> We are, during the winter, dreaming of Independence and Peace, without using the means to become so. In the Spring, when our Recruits should be with the Army and in training, we have just discovered the necessity of calling for them. and by the Fall, after a distressed, and inglorious campaign for want of them, we begin to get a few men which come in just time enough to eat our Provisions, and consume our Stores without rendering any service; that is, one year Rolls over another; and with out some change, we are hastening to our Ruin.[6]

Washington was describing the end of a winter at Morristown. He might have been describing winter's end at Valley Forge and the beginning of the Monmouth campaign. He was never as clear about his strategic situation and intentions as they applied to Monmouth, but his actions from 1776 to the end of the war spoke for him. Washington fought a full-scale battle against the concentrated force of the British army only once after 1776—in September 1777 at the battle of the Brandywine. He concluded that to risk battle was less dangerous than to damage morale by yielding Philadelphia—the capital—without a show of resistance. Predictably, on that occasion Washington's army lost the battle. He avoided major battles, preferring aggressive but small-scale strokes such as at Trenton, Princeton, Stony Point and Paulus Hook. He hoped thereby to sustain American morale and weaken the British will to persist. Rarely, as at Germantown, Washington risked an engagement on a somewhat larger scale. But on that occasion, much of the enemy army was occupied with the forts along the Delaware.

Against so consistent a strategic record of not putting "anything to the Risque, unless compelled by a necessity, into which we ought never to be drawn," there seems little reason to judge Washington's intentions at Monmouth as exceptional. Though the Monmouth campaign offered the opportunity for a major encounter with the British army, there is nothing in Washington's strategic record to indicate that he planned one. Misled by faulty intelligence, Washington seems to have misjudged the tactical situation and to have anticipated battle against an exposed and relatively weak enemy rear guard. General Lee's caution saved Washington from a dangerous betrayal of his own strategy. At Monmouth, Lee was more faithful than Washington to Washington's strategic design for the revolutionary war.

At Monmouth Washington intended merely to damage a vulnerable portion of the British army. Washington's strategy was never a Napoleonic one of climactic battles. Another small-scale American victory would both weaken the British government's will to persist and strengthen American resolve.

NOTES

1. Carl von Clausewitz, On War, trans. and ed. Michael Howard and Peter Paret (Princeton: Princeton University Press, 1976), bk. 2, chap. 1, p. 128.
2. Dave Richard Palmer, The Way of the Fox: American Strategy in the War for America, 1775-1783 (Westport, Conn.: Greenwood Press, 1975).
3. This succinct statement of Palmer's view of the third phase is from an article outlining his main arguments. Dave R. Palmer, "General George Washington: Grand Strategist or Mere Fabian?" Parameters: The Journal of the US Army War College, 4, no. 1 (1974): 1-16; quotation from p. 12.
4. Palmer, The Way of the Fox, p. 151.
5. George Washington to the President of Congress, September 8, 1776, John C. Fitzpatrick, ed., The Writings of George Washington from the Original Manuscript Sources, 1745-1799, 39 vols. (Washington, D.C.: U.S. Government Printing Office, 1931-44), 6:28.
6. Washington to John Augustine Washington, July 6, 1780, ibid., 19:136.

Lifting the Fog of Battle:
Charles Lee at the
Battie of Monmouth

Roy K. Flint

Studying the battle of Monmouth is a rewarding experience for two reasons. First, the unresolved issue of the competence and loyalty of Major General Charles Lee can still be debated. The culmination of this issue was the heated confrontation between General George Washington and Lee on the battlefield and the court-martial that followed. Since that time, historians have frequently castigated Lee for negligence or disloyalty and rarely praised him for his insights into the nature of the war in which he was engaged. Second, Monmouth is a pleasure for historiographical reasons. The proceedings of Lee's court-martial gives the historian an unusually complete oral history of the battle. This compendium of eyewitness accounts, assembled soon after the battle, provides an unusual opportunity to piece together a moment-by-moment reconstruction of the events of 28 June 1778. The numerous accounts of the battle also demonstrate once again how men react to the fear, noise, confusion, and the chaos of a battlefield through their varying descriptions of the same general experience. The "fog of battle" always presents a serious problem for both the commander in the field and for the historian who seeks to assess his performance.[1] One can never really be sure of having assembled and assessed all of the evidence correctly.

In trying to unravel the actions of Charles Lee and his command at the battle of Monmouth, one must grasp what Washington and Lee wanted to accomplish on that dreadfully hot day in 1778. The American and British armies had marched from Valley Forge and Philadelphia on converging axes and were headed for a collision. While Sir Henry Clinton was bent on withdrawing to Sandy Hook, Washington was moving to establish contact with his enemy. Washington kept the British army under surveillance and remained aware of its general location at all times. When the two armies drew near, it was Washington who sought to bring on battle. He had, in modern terms, conducted a "movement to contact," and he was about to open the action.

Although the dangers of evaluating the past by a modern standard are well known, we must establish criteria to measure Lee's performance. Since the study of current doctrine for movement to contact reveals certain tactical principles unaffected by the passage of time, that doctrine provides a legitimate way to evaluate Lee's and Washington's performance at Monmouth. Whether in 1778 or 1978, a land army groping for its enemy demonstrates the same characteristics. The commander sends out feelers to clarify an otherwise vague intelligence picture and then attempts to develop and reinforce the tactical situation to gain an advantage over the other side. This is what Washington wanted Lee to do on 28 June 1778.

Washington knew as early as the 26th that Clinton's army lay in the vicinity of Freehold. He also knew that he wanted to attack that army, bringing on an engagement to destroy at least a portion of the British force. To achieve this, Washington gave Lee command of an advance guard which was to move toward Freehold and concentrate on Clinton's left flank. In all, Lee had more than four thousand men under his immediate command, and was supported by Colonel Daniel Morgan's riflemen, operating against the British right flank, but out of contact with Lee. After spending the night of the 27th at Englishtown, Lee's force was to move forward early on the 28th to attack the British, whom Washington hoped to catch on the march. Washington proposed to follow with the main body so that he could support Lee once the latter was engaged.[2]

As is characteristic of a movement to contact, they had some idea of Clinton's strength—estimated at ten thousand men—but no exact information about the location or disposition of his forces at Freehold. Nor did they seem to understand fully the nature of the terrain around Freehold. By employing militia forces and infantry units in advanced positions, they hoped to collect the necessary intelligence. Further, because he lacked detailed information about the British, Lee did not make a complete plan on the evening of the 27th. As he told General Anthony Wayne, "the position of the enemy might render any previous plan invalid. . . ."[3] Lee contented himself with holding his detachment in readiness to move at a moment's notice.

After picking up local residents as guides, Lee moved out of Englishtown early on the 28th. He also sent Colonel William Grayson's regiment forward to scout the enemy and to maintain contact until the rest of the troops came up. Grayson's regiment, the militia of General Philemon Dickinson, and Morgan's riflemen comprised a covering force to provide information, give warning, and harass the enemy's small detachments.

After arriving at the bridge over Wemrock Creek, Lee divided his advance guard further by sending Wayne forward with a thousand men. By creating the advance party, Lee completed his organization for combat, providing security against surprise and flexibility for the attack. His covering force was to clarify the intelligence picture, and his advance party was to make the first serious contact. While committing the smaller force first and withholding the bulk of his troops, Lee retained the ability to move the advance guard freely to reinforce Wayne's detachment once contact was made. Similarly, Lee's entire command was to perform the same service for Washington as the commander in chief sought the right spot to strike the British with his main body. This formation was supposed to provide rapid development of a battle and gain Washington an advantage over the enemy.

As Wayne's men advanced toward Monmouth Court House and then in the direction of Briar Hill, information about the enemy remained confused. Conflicting reports insisted that the British were on the march and that they had not yet moved. Lee quite correctly moved forward "determined to march on and ascertain with my own eyes, the number, order, and disposition of the enemy, and conduct myself accordingly."[4] To complicate matters, he found that his troops had to cross three "morasses," the first of which was spanned by a single bridge. Any one of these obstacles could have made him vulnerable to attack while his forces were divided. Washington's position, still some seven miles away—out of supporting distance should he be needed— made Lee's situation all the more precarious.

Pressing forward, Wayne's advance party made contact with the British rear guard near Briar Hill. After Wayne broke a British cavalry charge, Lee's tactical situation took a turn for the worse. British strength to the east began to build, and the enemy advanced against his right flank. Simultaneously units in the vicinity of Wayne's position began to withdraw without orders, apparently triggered by the rearward movement of Lieutenant Colonel Eleazar Oswald's artillery battery. Lee quickly perceived that growing enemy strength to his front and on his right endangered his advance guard. And still Washington's main body had not arrived.

Despite Wayne's protests, Lee tried to organize a rearward defensive position which he soon had to abandon. Lacking effective communication with the elements of his command, Lee was unable to control the withdrawal and retire in an orderly manner. At this point he was confronted by the irate Washington who had preceded the main body, and Lee's day of battle came to an end.

How well had Lee done? Considering the tactical role he had to play, how well had he performed the responsibilities of an advance guard commander in a movement to contact? Lee had made the only practical plan, for with the information at hand and in the time available no more detailed scheme was possible. He had moved early and quickly to the Freehold area, assumed the proper formation and placed one of his best fighting generals in command of the van. He had tried personally to gain information about the enemy when conflicting reports obscured the situation. To this point no one could expect more from an advance guard commander.

But Washington wanted a victory, and Lee did not give him one. For this Washington is to some degree responsible, for he failed to arrive on the battlefield with the main body at the moment when Lee needed his support. Instead, outnumbered, Lee fell back under pressure of the aggressive Clinton. Even in his withdrawal—however ragged it may have been—Lee's actions were consistent with the orders he had received and the mission of an advance guard commander in a movement to contact. He reacted correctly, if not with parade ground precision, to the threatening situation that he saw developing in his front and particularly on his right flank. When the foggy picture of the enemy finally cleared, Lee found that his best course of action was to defend himself, contain the enemy, and await the arrival of Washington.

NOTES

1. The principal source for any study of the battle of Monmouth is the Proceedings of a General Court-Martial . . . for the Trial of Major General Lee, July 4th, 1778 (New York, 1864). This remarkable document is, except for map support, a complete record of the battle. Nevertheless, there are excellent secondary sources to assist the investigation by filling in some of the remaining gaps. Among those consulted were John Richard Alden's General Charles Lee: Traitor or Patriot? (Baton Rouge: Louisiana State University Press, 1951); Samuel S. Smith's The Battle of Monmouth (Monmouth Beach, N.J.: Philip Freneau Press, 1964); and Theodore Thayer's The Making of a Scapegoat: Washington and Lee at Monmouth (Port Washington, N.Y.: Kennikat Press, 1976). In addition, John W. Shy contributes a convincing interpretation of Lee as a soldier in his revised essay "American Strategy: Charles Lee and the Radical Alternative," in his A People Numerous and Armed (New York: Oxford University Press, 1976). Maps that depicted the battlefield and the movement of units accurately were particularly hard to find. The author relied on the one found on page 55 of Henry B. Carrington's Battle Maps and Charts of the American Revolution (New York: A.S. Barnes, 1881) which seemed best supported by the testimony found in the Proceedings of a General Court-Martial. Contemporary doctrine for movement to contact was taken from U.S. Department of the Army, FM 71-100, Brigade and Division Operations (March 1977), the latest field manual that covers a formation comparable to Lee's.

2. Brigadier General Anthony Wayne's testimony, Proceedings of a General Court-Martial, p. 8.

3. Ibid., p. 7.

4. Major General Lee's testimony, ibid., p. 205.

The Traitorcus Charles Lee

Kemble Widmer

I am not an expert on the battle of Monmouth, having had more to do with the battles of Trenton and Princeton. I haven't had an opportunity to do much arguing with Sam Smith about Monmouth although I've wanted to for many years. Sam and I have fought the battle of Princeton in my Pennington living room until my wife thought we'd come to blows.

I know the problem is complicated, but from my reading of the evidence, Charles Lee was a traitor. I know that is not a popular position in Monmouth County. It's like my old history professor at Lehigh University used to say. "Gentlemen," said Professor Lawrence Henry Gipson, "if you had lived at the time of the American Revolution, you'd all be Tories." And if I read my New Jersey history right, there were an awful lot of Tories in Monmouth County.

I think Lee was a traitor as early as 1776. Whether this was because of his own ambition or some defect of his character I don't know. But an intelligence officer friend of mine wondered why one side or the other hadn't strung him up by the neck long before the British captured him at Basking Ridge. My friend thought Lee's capture was clearly such a put up job that any intelligence officer could recognize it for what it was.

Charles Lee was allegedly a very competent commander. In December 1776 he knew the British were concerned about his army operating on their flank and rear as they chased Washington through New Jersey. He must have presumed that British patrols would be looking for him. (Apparently they weren't.) So supposedly against his better judgment he bivouacked outside his lines, and then blamed his capture on the "rascals" of his own army. The patrol that captured Lee on the night of December 12-13, 1776, was the only long-distance patrol the British had sent out in weeks. It just happened to arrive in the same town Lee was visiting at precisely the time he was there. They made this meeting look good by killing a few Americans, taking Lee to New York strapped to his horse, and loudly threatening to string him up. This was all to look convincing to Washington's intelligence. When one realizes that the patrol started the day before and headed for the one area in all of New Jersey where a former officer of the regiment was violating his own rules of security, an unplanned meeting seems unlikely.

You have already heard Dr. Ryan describe Lee's treasonable activities while a British captive. But I would remind you that what Lee did in retreat across New Jersey in 1776 was very similar to what he did, in a more compressed time, at Monmouth in 1778. In the court-martial proceedings, officers of every rank said that Washington did not order Lee to attack Clinton. Washington told Lee to use his own good judgment. While the orders may not have included latitude for an all-out assault, Lee was directed to attack and harass the British column. Alexander Hamilton summarized it best by saying (and I'm paraphrasing) that he could not conceive of Washington giving a specific order to attack, but that he gave senior officers the latitude to do what a given situation demanded. In short, in both the retreat across New Jersey and at Monmouth, Lee delayed in complying with Washington's requests for prompt action because he did not agree with his commander's planned objectives.

Now, as to my learned colleagues this morning. Dr. Lender has stated that General Clinton rested his troops at Freehold, waiting—and hoping—for Washington to attack him. I don't believe any such thing. Clinton halted to get his baggage train in order, and then had to pass the twelve-mile-long caravan through his army and on its way to the Navesink Highlands and favorable defensive terrain. He sent his Hessians, who weren't involved at Monmouth, to guard the baggage and supplies.

I wonder what would have happened if Lee had waited to hold his council of war until he'd received better intelligence reports. Instead, his meeting early on the evening of June 27 was based on inadequate information. He just sort of let things ride, saying he'd develop a plan in the morning—in effect, that he'd improvise. One of the reasons Lee gave for his retreat was unfavorable terrain. Not necessarily so. For example, Wayne and his advance group got into a little tangle with British cavalry. He managed to repulse the enemy because his troops were screened by woods and supported by riflemen. As an aside, Wayne was deathly afraid of facing British cavalry in open ground with American infantry. The British were equally afraid of the American riflemen, particularly on broken ground. There were favorable features to the terrain, specifically the many wooded areas and numerous small ravines which prevented the British from maneuvering their infantry in the accustomed parade ground manner and restricted their use of cavalry.

Many scholars, for example Colonel Flint, contend that Washington was too far away to lend support. I don't read the trial testimony quite that way. Washington was coming up fast and Lee had already managed to hold the British off for more than an hour. If Lee had used the good tactical judgment he had previously demonstrated, he certainly could have reinforced Wayne. His retreat seems unnecessary given Washington's approach with the main army. Lee could instead have led Cornwallis off to the northeast, toward New Brunswick.

Many scholars have criticized my evaluation of Lee. They have also criticized Washington's inaction until he "formed the line," and rallied Lee's troops. Washington's inaction may have been due to his belief that Lee was in command of the situation. He acted when he found this was not the case.

As the court martial proceedings make clear, although Washington's orders were vague, Lee did understand them. He did not approve of their purpose. So he failed to devise suitable tactics for their implementation. In consequence, he allowed his subordinate commanders to act independently. It should be noted that Washington said Lee should have refused the command if he didn't think he could do the job. I wonder how many British would lie in the cemeteries around here, instead of Americans, if Wayne or Greene had been in charge instead of Lee.

THEY WERE THERE:
THE BATTLE OF MONMOUTH
THROUGH PARTICIPANTS' EYES.
A SELECTED BIBLIOGRAPHY
OF PRINTED SOURCES

Robert F. Van Benthuysen

The printed literature dealing with the battle of Monmouth is ample, and since I prefer to think of the battle more as a campaign than as a single event, my choice of literature reflects this. The campaign began with the British evacuation of Philadelphia and the nearly simultaneous departure of the American troops from Valley Forge, and includes the convergent journeys of the two armies, the battle itself, the embarkation of the British troops for New York at Sandy Hook on July 5, 1778, and the court-martial of Charles Lee.

The body of literature about the Monmouth campaign includes monographs, pamphlets, journal articles, newspaper accounts, official records, and even a great deal of eulogistic poetry of questionable quality, but unquestionable sincerity. But it is on first person accounts of the campaign that this essay concentrates: American, British and Hessian memoirs, diaries, journals and letters. Some were written in the field, while the smoke of battle literally hung in the air, and convey a stirring sense of immediacy. At least one account was written fifty years after the battle. Some writers incorporated materials from other sources and go beyond eyewitness accounts. All should be read with caution; they contain inaccuracies of fact and biases growing out of the partisan feelings of their authors.

American Participants

The most comprehensive primary source covering the Monmouth campaign, as well as the revolutionary war in general, is The Writings of George Washington from the Original Manuscript Sources, 1745-1799, edited by John C. Fitzpatrick and published in thirty-nine volumes by the U.S. Government Printing Office between 1931 and 1944. Material pertaining to the battle of Monmouth is found in volume twelve, pages 75-147. It is from this source that we learn not only of Washington's strategic concerns, but of his immersion in the daily minutiae of the management of an army. On the day before the battle, for example, he wrote to General Horatio Gates: "I think you are right in reducing the rations of meat and increasing it in flour and rice. Our supplies of the former are scarce and difficult to obtain of the latter they are plenty and easy" (12:125).

A full account of the battle, filled with conflicting testimony by participants, is Proceedings of a General Court-Martial, held at Brunswick in the State of New-Jersey, by Order of His Excellency Gen. Washington . . . for the Trial of Major-General Lee, July 4th, 1778. John Dunlap, printer of Philadelphia, brought out a 62-page edition of 100 copies, authorized by

Congress, in 1778. In 1823 a 134-page version was published at Cooperstown, New York, by J.H. Prentiss. It was privately reprinted in New York in 1864. The account is repetitive, but very compelling, and Lee comes across as a most astute, if ultimately futile advocate of his own cause.

A number of the items in The Lee Papers, correspondence by and to the general, as well as other material he wrote, concern the Monmouth campaign. The four volumes of The Lee Papers are the Collections of the New-York Historical Society . . . for the years 1871-74 and were published in 1872-75. Volume three contains the proceedings of Lee's court-martial.

The first volume of The Papers of Alexander Hamilton, edited by Harold C. Syrett, contains Hamilton's letter to Elias Boudinot in which Hamilton, a participant in the battle, criticizes Lee. He said "this man is either a driveler in the field of soldiership or something much worse . . . his conduct was monstrous and unpardonable" (pp. 510, 514). Hamilton lauds Washington for the manner in which he dealt with Lee's retreating troops:

> I never saw the General to so much advantage. His coolness and firmness were admirable. He instantly took measures for checking the enemy's advance. America owes a great deal to General Washington for this day's work; a general route [rout] dismay and disgrace would have attended the whole army in any other hands but his. By his own good sense and fortitude he turned the fate of the day (1:512).

The Hamilton papers are published by Columbia University Press, 26 volumes to date.

The Revolutionary War Journals of Henry Dearborn, 1775-1783 contain a few pages on Monmouth. Dearborn, a lieutenant colonel, is impersonal and objective. He rarely philosophizes and wastes little space in damning the enemy. Casually he relates the advance of his men:

> When they [the British] found we ware about to attact them they formed & stood Redy to Receive us, when we ariv'd within 200 yards of them we form.d Batallion & advanc'd but having two Rail fences to take Down as we advanced, (the Last of which was within 60 yards of the Enimy) we Could advance but slowly, the Enimy when we ware takeing Down the Last fence, give us a very heavy fire which we Did not Return (pp. 127-28).

Dearborn thought so much of his experiences during the battle that he later named his grant of land in Maine, "Monmouth." The journals were edited by Lloyd A. Brown and Howard H. Peckham and published by Books for Libraries Press in 1969.

In addition to descriptions of the battle by officers, we are fortunate to have the well-known account by a Continental army private, Joseph Plumb Martin's A Narrative of Some of the Adventures, Dangers, and Sufferings of a Revolutionary Soldier: Interspersed with Anecdotes of Incidents that Occurred within his own Observations, Written by Himself. . . , originally printed in 1830 and frequently reprinted. Martin's account is graphic, intimately detailed and absorbing. During his seven years of service Martin saw Washington twice: at Monmouth and again at Yorktown. His recollection of Washington's encounter with Lee quotes Washington as saying "damn him," and became the source of much later discussion about what Washington actually did say to Lee on that occasion. Martin also recounts the story of "Molly Pitcher" and the cannonball, quoted above in its entirety by Elizabeth Evans.

Other American accounts of the battle include Alexander Hamilton, "The Battle of Monmouth. Letters of Alexander Hamilton and General William Irvine, Describing the Engagement," Pennsylvania Magazine of History and Biography, v. 2, no. 2 (1878): 139-48; John Laurens, The Army Correspondence of Colonel John Laurens in the Years 1777-8, . . . (1867; New York: Arno Press, 1969); James McHenry, "The Battle of Monmouth, Described by Dr. James McHenry, Secretary to General Washington," Magazine of American History, 3 (1879): 355-63; James McHenry, Journal of a March, a Battle and a Watchfall, Being the Versions Elaborated by James McHenry from His Diary of the Year 1778, Begun at Valley Forge and Containing Accounts of the British, the Indians and the battle of Monmouth (Greenwich, Conn.: privately printed, 1945); Robert Morris, "Letters of Chief Justice Morris, 1777-79," Proceedings of the New Jersey Historical Society, New Series, v. 5, no. 3 (July 1920): 168-78 (containing one letter describing the battle and of interest chiefly because it was written by a noncombatant); Jeremiah Greenman, Diary of a Common Soldier in the American Revolution, 1775-1783, ed. Robert C. Bray and Paul E. Bushnell (DeKalb, Ill.: Northern Illinois University Press, 1978); and the second volume of The Papers of William Livingston, ed. Carl E. Prince and Dennis P. Ryan (Trenton: New Jersey Historical Commission, 1980).

British Participants

The British commander in chief, Sir Henry Clinton, summarized the battle of Monmouth as follows:

> The rear guard of the King's army is attacked on its march by the avant garde of the enemy. It turns upon them, drives them, drives them back to their gross, remains some hours in their presence until all its advanced detachments return, and then falls back, without being followed, to the ground from which the enemy had been first driven, where it continues for several hours undisturbed waiting for the cool of the evening to resume its march (p. 97).

Clinton's account, The American Rebellion, Sir Henry Clinton's Narrative of His Campaigns, 1775-1782 (ed. William B. Willcox; New Haven: Yale University Press, 1954), was written with the advantage, and the distortion, of hindsight. He had a copy of Lee's court-martial and refers to it several times in his reconstruction of the battle.

Other British sources include K.G. Davies ed., Documents of the American Revolution, 1770-1783, Colonial Office Series (Shannon: Irish University Press, 1976); vol. 15, pp. 159-63, deals with Monmouth. Andrew Bell, "Copy of a Journal of Andrew Bell, Esq., at One Time Confidential Secretary of General Sir Henry Clinton . . . ," Proceedings of the New Jersey Historical Society, v. 6, no. 1 (1851): 15-19; John Andre, Major Andre's Journal; Operations of the British Army under Lieutenant Generals Sir William Howe and Sir Henry Clinton, June 1777 to November 1778 . . . (1904, 1930; New York: Arno Press, 1968); Stephen Kemble, The Kemble Papers, 2 vols., 1884-85 (Collections of the New-York Historical Society, vols. 16-17);

Kemble was adjutant general and deputy adjutant general of the British army in North America, 1772-79; Archibald Robertson, Lieutenant-General Royal Engineers. His Diaries and Sketches in America 1762-1780, ed. Harry Miller Lydenberg (1930; New York: Arno Press, 1971); and John Graves Simcoe, Simcoe's Military Journal. A History of the Operations of a Partisan Corps, Called the Queen's Rangers . . . (1844; New York: Arno Press, 1968).

Hessian Participants

The first two sources below give especially good descriptions of the British march across New Jersey from Philadelphia, including much on "lewdry," looting, and accounts of desertions by British and Hessian troops. Carl Leopold Baurmeister, Revolution in America: Confidential Letters and Journals, 1776-1784 . . . , trans. and annot. Bernhard A. Uhlendorf (New Brunswick: Rutgers University Press, 1957), and John Charles Philip de Krafft, Journal of Lieutenant John Charles von Kraft, 1776-1784 (1883; Collections of the New-York Historical Society for 1882, v. 12; New York: Arno Press, 1968). Also of interest is Johann Ewald's Diary of the American War: A Hessian Journal, trans. and ed. Joseph P. Tustin (New Haven, Conn.: Yale University Press, 1979).

ABOUT THE CONTRIBUTORS

ELIZABETH EVANS, a New York based freelance writer, achieved national renown in 1975 for her book Weathering the Storm: Women of the American Revolution, a comprehensive view of the triumphs and sufferings of women on both sides of the Revolutionary War. Ms. Evans is an active member of the American Revolution Round Table, serving on its Board of Governors.

COLONEL ROY K. FLINT is Professor and Head, Department of History, United States Military Academy, West Point, New York. Colonel Flint, in more than a quarter century in the Army, has had broad combat and command experience.

MARK EDWARD LENDER is Director of Grants at Kean College of New Jersey and Editor of New Jersey History. He is also an associate member of the graduate faculty in history at Rutgers University. Lender is author of The New Jersey Soldier (1975), The River War: The Fight for the Delaware, 1777 (1979), and, with James Kirby Martin, coauthor of "A Respectable Army": The Military Origins of the Republic, 1763-1789 (1982) and Drinking In America: A History (1982).

JAMES KIRBY MARTIN is professor and chairman of the Department of History, University of Houston, University Park. His writings on the social and military aspects of the revolutionary era include Men in Rebellion: Higher Governmental Leaders and the Coming of the American Revolution (1973); In the Course of Human Events: An Interpretive Exploration of the American Revolution (1979); and A Respectable Army: The Military Origins of the Republic, 1763-1789 (1982, with Mark E. Lender).

DENNIS P. RYAN is adjunct associate professor of history, New York University, and co-editor of the Papers of William Livingston. He is editor of A Salute to Courage: The American Revolution as Seen Through Wartime Writings of Officers of the Continental Army and Navy (1979).

SAMUEL S. SMITH is one of New Jersey's foremost historians, specializing in military history. His books include The Battle of Monmouth (1964), The Battle of Trenton (1965), The Battle of Princeton (1967), and Fight for the Delaware, 1777 (1970), The Battle of Brandywine (1976), Winter at Morristown 1779-1780, The Darkest Hour (1979), and a biography, Lewis Moore, Anglo-American Statesmen, ca. 1619-1691 (1983).

ROBERT F. VAN BENTHUYSEN is director of the Murry and Leonie Guggenheim Memorial Library, Monmouth College, West Long Branch, New Jersey. He is an expert on Monmouth County and New Jersey history and on the manuscript and printed resources for the study of that history.

RUSSELL F. WEIGLEY is professor of history at Temple University and a widely respected military historian. His books include <u>Towards an American Army: Military Thought from Washington to Marshall</u> (1962, 1974), <u>A History of the United States Army</u> (1967); <u>The American Way of War: A History of United States Military Strategy and Policy</u> (1973); and <u>Eisenhower's Lieutenants: The Campaign of France and Germany, 1944-1945</u> (1981).

KEMBLE WIDMER, former State Geologist

of New Jersey, is a retired Colonel in the Army Reserve, a graduate of Command and General Staff School and a visiting lecturer at the U.S. Military Academy, West Point, New York. He has studied the military history of the American Revolution as an avocation for many years. A popular speaker throughout the state, he is author of <u>The Christmas Campaign: The Ten Days of Trenton and Princeton</u> (1975).